CELTIC WISDOM

❖

SEASONAL FESTIVALS
AND RITUALS

CELTIC
WISDOM

SEASONAL FESTIVALS
AND RITUALS

VIVIANNE CROWLEY

A GODSFIELD BOOK

Library of Congress Cataloging-in-Publication Data Available

10 9 8 7 6 5 4 3 2 1

Published in 1998 by Sterling Publishing Company, Inc.
387 Park Avenue South, New York, N.Y. 10016

DESIGNED AND EDITED BY
THE BRIDGEWATER BOOK COMPANY LTD

Designer *Stephen Minns*
Editor *Antonia Maxwell*
Picture research *Vanessa Fletcher*
Illustrations *Lorraine Harrison, Sarah Young*
Studio Photography *Ian Parsons*

Distributed in Canada by Sterling Publishing
c/o Canadian Manda Group, One Atlantic Avenue, Suite 105
Toronto, Ontario, Canada M6K 3E7
Distributed in Australia by Capricorn Link (Australia) Pty Ltd
P O. Box 6651, Baulkham Hills, Business Centre, NSW 2153, Australia

Printed and bound in Hong Kong

ISBN 0-8069-7056-1

ACKNOWLEDGMENT

Corn Craft, Monks Eleigh, Ipswich, Suffolk

TITLE PAGE *Stonehenge, Wiltshire, England*

RIGHT *"King Arthur's Wedding Feast,"*
1905, Arthur Rackham (1867–1939)

CONTENTS

INTRODUCTION

This is a book of Celtic Wisdom, but perhaps we should start by asking: who are the Celts? They are the descendants of a number of migratory tribes with common roots whose culture spread across Europe. Before the expansion of the Roman Empire, they were one of the most powerful peoples of Europe. Celtic kingdoms flourished from Germany down to modern Spain and from Ireland to as far East as what is now Turkey. In the years before Christianity, the Celts suffered many setbacks. Many tribes were conquered by the organized discipline of the Roman army. Later, after the Roman Empire collapsed, the Celts were forced to the far west of Europe by invading Germanic tribes. The main Celtic homelands of Europe are now Ireland, Scotland, Wales, the Isle of Man, Cornwall in southwest England, Brittany in northwest France and Galicia in northwest Spain.

CELTIC REVIVAL

In recent centuries, the Celtic nations have been ruled and colonized by England, France, and Spain. Their languages were supressed through compulsory schooling, which forced children to speak the languages of their governments and to forget their own heritage. Thankfully, this era is coming to an end. All the Celtic nations are experiencing a cultural revival. There are also Europe-wide initiatives to help stimulate Celtic culture, such as the annual Celtic Film Festival, which encourages directors to make films in Celtic languages. There are two main groups of Celtic languages. Scottish Gaelic, Manx, and Irish are closely related and form one group. Welsh, Breton, and Cornish form the other.

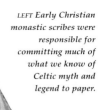

LEFT Early Christian monastic scribes were responsible for committing much of what we know of Celtic myth and legend to paper.

The Irish government has successfully revitalized the Irish language, which all schoolchildren must learn. All official communications are in both languages and there are Irish-language radio and television channels. Through the popularity of groups such as Clannad, we hear Irish sung throughout the world

In Scotland, new technology links are bringing work to the Gaelic-speaking Highlands and Islands. These opportunities mean that people can find well-paid jobs while remaining in their traditional culture. Their Gaelic language is more likely to survive and new generations are born with Gaelic as their first language.

Welsh has continued to be the first language of large areas of Wales. Education is bilingual. Both languages are used for all official purposes and there are also dedicated Welsh-language television and radio channels.

In England, Cornwall in the southwest is the county that has remained most Celtic. People no longer speak Cornish as an everyday language, but poetry is being written and films made in Cornish. Until the 1950s, the French government took strong punitive measures against the Breton language.

ABOVE *The ninth-century Macgregor gospel, from Ireland, contains a broad range of beautifully executed traditional Celtic motifs and symbols.*

Children who spoke Breton at school were beaten. There has since been a language revival, though not without a struggle. Most road signs in Brittany are now in Breton and French, and Breton is being taught in some schools. Cultural centers are active and teach traditional dance, songs, music, and poetry to new generations whose parents cannot speak Breton. There is a huge Inter-Celtic music festival each year at Lorient, near the famous megalith site of Carnac. This brings together musicians from all the Celtic nations. Contact with Ireland and groups such as the Chieftains has stimulated Breton music and musicians such as Breton singer and harpist Alain Stivell have achieved worldwide fame.

ACROSS THE WATERS

Of course, Celtic migration did not stop in Europe. Centuries of colonialism by the larger European nations created a legacy of poverty and oppression in the Celtic nations. The Celts left their homelands in their millions, seeking work and freedom. The great migrations of the eighteenth, nineteenth, and twentieth centuries mean that many citizens of the United States, English- and French-speaking Canada, Australia, and New Zealand can all trace their roots back to a Celtic ancestry.

Though far from their ancestors' homelands, Celtic culture and wisdom speak to the hearts and memories of those of Celtic ancestry. How many spirits do not thrill when we hear echoing through the halls of ancestral memory the bagpipes' wail? How many of us do not have tears in our eyes when we watch New York's St. Patrick's Day Parade? How many of us can resist the impulse to clap our hands and tap our feet when we see the passion of Irish dance brought to life again by Michael Flatley and by Riverdance?

LEFT The legendary Celtic hero Vercingetorix was one of the last rebels to be crushed by the advancing Roman army in central Gaul in 53BC.

OPPOSITE The landscape of the Celtic nations continues to inspire poetry and music.

CELTIC SPIRITUALITY

In their migrations across Europe and beyond, the Celts did not bring just themselves, they also brought their myths and legends—a strange wild and mysterious tapestry of heroes, heroines, goddesses, gods, custom, superstition, magic, folk tradition, and spirituality, both Christian and preChristian.

In the preChristian era, the Pagan Celts had evolved a highly developed culture and spirituality. The guardians of Celtic tradition were the Druids who were priests, bards, judges, philosophers, and advisers to the rulers. Druids were revered and could walk the most savage battlefield unharmed. They were the living libraries of their peoples, for the Celts considered spiritual teachings to be too sacred to write down. These were learned by heart at Druidic colleges where students might study for up to twenty years. Each Celtic tribe had its own deity. There were also deities whose worship was more widely spread and who presided over every aspect of life from the arts to warfare. Some goddesses and gods are known to us today, but others are not. The Celts were careful to guard the names of their deities.

SPIRITUALITY TODAY

Followers of Celtic spirituality today draw on a number of different Celtic traditions. Druidry has reemerged all over the Western world, but particularly in England, Wales, Brittany, and North America. There are now many Druid orders actively teaching Celtic lore and spirituality. Others

ABOVE Recovered Celtic artifacts, such as the famous Gündestrup Cauldron, found in 1891 in Denmark, have taught us much of what we know of the beliefs and way of life of these ancient people.

follow Wicca or Celtic Witchcraft. This is not the Witchcraft of Black Masses and Devil-worship, but the true WiseCraft of the land. It is a Medicine Way and Blessing Way that honors the ancient deities and practices magic, healing, and the **sight**, those latent psychic abilities that are so much part of Celtic heritage.

CELTIC CHRISTIANITY

Others have not discarded Christianity but have returned to the early Celtic Christianity that preceded both Roman Catholicism and Protestantism in the far west of Europe.

Christianity came early to the Celtic lands and found in the hospitable Celtic tradition a home from persecution. Christianity and Druidry did not always welcome each other, but there was much fusion between the two faiths. Celtic deities became Celtic saints. In Brittany, the horned God Cernunnos became Saint Cornelly, patron saint of cattle and Mother Goddess Ana became Saint Anne of Brittany, the grandmother of Jesus. In Ireland and Scotland, the Goddess Brigid or Bridget, who was also known as Bride and Brigantia, became Saint Bridget. Celtic Christianity developed a spiritual tradition of learning that was the inheritor of its Druid ancestor, in which both women and men were spiritual leaders.

The separate development of Celtic Christianity was encouraged by the collapse of the Roman Empire which left it largely cut off from developments in the Roman Catholic Church. The Celtic Church continued to use Latin for its masses and sacraments, but its flourishing monasteries produced volumes of literature in Irish and other languages of the people. This literature showed much continuity between the spirituality of Christianity and earlier Pagan traditions. In particular the Celtic Church retained the Celtic attitude to Nature.

The horned man, simultaneously a wild and pagan figure and a symbol of fertility and renewed life, is shown on the Gündestrup Cauldron clutching a serpent in one hand and a magical torque in the other.

THE SACRED LAND

Traditionally Roman Catholicism and Protestantism have not been friendly to Nature. They have taught that human beings have dominion over the Earth and that her resources are here for us to exploit. We can ignore the reality of our ecological crisis by telling ourselves that the world is about to end. If we believe this, it does not matter that our rivers and seas are so polluted that our fish die. We need not worry that multinational corporations cut down our forests to graze cattle for burgers and that our climate is altered irrevocably. We can "eat, drink, and be merry, for tomorrow we die."

This was not the attitude of the ancient Celts to their environment. Celtic society was similar in many ways to that of Native American peoples. The world of Nature and the world of the Divine were inseparable. Nature and the starry realms beyond were the garment of the Divine. These ancient peoples considered everything around them to be sacred. The Earth on which they walked, each hill and standing stone was holy; so too were sky and Sun, Moon, and star. They gave honor to the springs of fresh water that brought health and healing. They reverenced the great ocean that brought fish to feed their families and over which they could voyage to the mysterious lands of the West.

LEFT The Celts saw in nature a manifestation of the Divine, and, even after the arrival of Christianity, many of their sacred rites and practices took place outside in honor of the beauty and perfection they saw there.

OPPOSITE Many ancient stones still standing today have connections to a distant past and Druidic rites, such as the Great Orme, or Maen Sigl.

NATURE AND THE DIVINE

As children, many of us sense that Nature is sacred. As we grow up, some of us forget, but some do not. We may find that the God we worship in our city temples and churches is not the Divinity who speaks to us in our dreams and visions. Spontaneously, we turn our prayers to the Mother Goddess, or to the Gods of forest, hill, and stream. We sense that behind the garment of Nature is the in-dwelling presence of the Divine.

To our Celtic ancestors it was obvious and natural that the world of Nature should be a gateway to the spiritual realm. To worship the Divine in a building made by human hands was not traditional for the Celts. Even with the coming of Christianity, they did not build mighty cathedrals. These were the work of the later Roman Church. Celtic Christian communities built tiny chapels and prayed by seashores caressed by clean unpolluted waves while listening to the cry of the gulls. They prayed in the silence of a forest glade to the sound of bird song. They meditated seated on the green grassy mound of an ancient burial chamber while plucking the strings of a harp.

ABOVE *Contemplation of ancient Celtic deities, such as Brigid, traditionally regarded as goddess of metalwork, poetic inspiration, and therapy, link us to our past and to a universal truth.*

A CELTIC JOURNEY

This book is a journey through the cycle of Nature drawing on the ancient wisdom of the Celts. There are many paths to the Divine and there is a timeless wisdom in all spiritual traditions. It should not surprise us if the words of a Celtic bard should speak of the same truths as a Native American chief, a Christian mystic, or the Buddha. Human spiritual truths are universal and represent a reaching out from our individual selves to the greater whole. They are about connection with our immediate friends and family, with society, and with the cosmos—the world of Nature and the universe beyond.

PRESENT NOT PAST

Though wisdom is universal, for those of Celtic ancestry, the Celtic traditions speak at a deep level to our hearts, minds, and spirits. Even if we were not born in the Celtic lands, the Celtic traditions are part of us and we are part of them. However, it is important to remember that we are not ancient

Celts. We seek to attune ourselves to the ways of our ancestors, but we are not harking back to some romantic reconstruction of the past. There is much in ancient Celtic culture that we have now evolved beyond. The Celtic love of warfare and headhunting, and their practices of keeping slaves, are not activities we are seeking to revive today. We look to the wisdom of the past so that we can live better in the present and future; but we act with discernment. We discard what is worn out. We bring forward to the future that which is useful. Let us now turn to the seasonal cycle of the Celts.

BELOW **Modern Druidic rites are rooted in the past, but their worship and traditions transcend history and culture and represent timeless, universal truths.**

THE FESTIVALS

The Celtic year was divided into eight stations, according to the movement and position of the Sun. Each station was marked by a festival, in which the passing of the old season and the arrival of the new was celebrated. The Celts lived in an agricultural society and their survival depended on an intimate understanding of the seasons and their changes. The yearly cycle of life, death, and rebirth was honored and celebrated in the hope of its continuation. In modern society we have lost our link to this natural cycle, living by artificial time and off mass produced food. By bringing the ancient beliefs and sacred rites of our forebears into our lives again, we can hope to regain our connection with the universe and with the essence of life itself.

The movement of the Sun was fundamental to the Celtic year, and many of the stone monuments that marked its transit have survived to the present day. The most famous of these is Stonehenge in Wiltshire, England, which is still a focal point for modern Druidic Solstice rites.

We can honor the Divine anywhere and at any time, but in all spiritual traditions there are special times and tides for celebration. Festivals act as important reminders. In our busy modern lives when we juggle jobs, studying, parenting, and relationships, it can be all too easy to neglect the spiritual realm. Our spirituality is important. To develop a spiritual life is not to turn away from everyday reality, but to renew our inner strength and resources so that we can better live our lives in the world.

In traditions such as Christianity and Islam that follow the revelations of a single prophet, religious festivals are usually based around incidents in the prophet's life. In Judaism, festivals are based around important events in the history of the Jewish people. In Celtic and in other ancient traditions, festivals are based around the cycle of Nature.

THE WHEEL OF THE YEAR

Our knowledge of the Celtic calendar derives from historical records and from archaeological finds such as the Coligny calendar. This was engraved on a large bronze tablet discovered in the French town of Coligny near Bourg-en-Bresse in 1897. We also find vestiges of the festivals in folk traditions and seasonal customs that have continued into the present or recent past.

Those who follow a Celtic spiritual tradition today celebrate eight seasonal festivals. These take place at roughly equidistant points throughout the year. The eight festivals are often known as "The Wheel of the Year." The wheel was an important symbol in Celtic mythology. It represented the turning of the Sun and the wheel of rebirth.

ABOVE *The Wheel of the Year symbolizes the constant change of the universe and the infinite cycle of birth, death, and rebirth.*

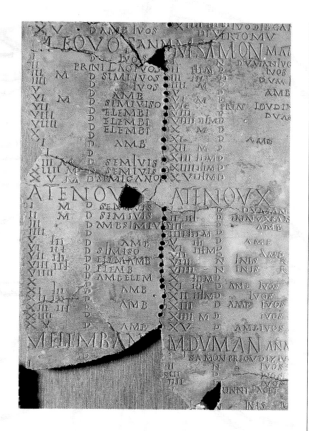

LEFT *The ancient bronze tablet, named the Coligny calendar after the French town in which it was discovered in 1897, has provided us with much of what we now know of the Celtic year.*

EARLY FESTIVALS

Celtic festivals, like Jewish festivals, begin at sunset on the evening before the main festival day and end at sunset on the following day.

The earliest Celts may have celebrated only two major festivals—Samhain on October 31/November 1, the beginning of winter, and Beltane on April 30/May 1, the beginning of summer. Over the millennia, other festivals evolved into the eight we celebrate today.

Some festivals mark important stages in the life of cattlerearing people. Beltane is when cattle can be taken up into the hills and mountains to summer grazing lands. Samhain is when they are brought down again and those which cannot be fed through the winter are slaughtered.

The festival of Imbolc on January 31/February 1 marks the beginning of the spring lambing season when ewes begin to produce milk. This was important both for supplying new sources of meat but also because milk would be available to make cheese. Lughnasadh on July 31/August 1 was originally the major summer cattle fair. Later, when the Celts began to develop agriculture, it became a harvest celebration as well.

SOLSTICES AND EQUINOXES

The dates of the Solstices and Equinoxes can vary slightly because of fluctuations in the Earth's orbit, but usually Spring Equinox is from March 20 to 21, Summer Solstice from June 21 to 22, Autumn Equinox from September 21 to 22 and Winter Solstice from December 21 to 22.

ABOVE The famous holed stone of Men-an-Tol in Cornwall, England, is oriented to catch the Sun at the Spring Equinox, and, along with many other such monuments, testifies to the central part the movement of the Sun played in the agricultural year.

Summer Solstice is the longest day of the year and Winter Solstice is the shortest day. In modern Druidry, Summer Solstice is known as **Alban Heruin** and Winter Solstice as **Alban Arthuan**. The Celts may not have celebrated the Solstices until they migrated to western Europe. There they encountered earlier cultures who used the stone circles and burial chambers that covered the landscape to calculate the exact moment of the longest and shortest days. Burial chambers and stone circles were constructed so the sunrise would strike on particular stones on these days. This enabled an accurate calendar to be calculated.

We have no evidence that the ancient Celts celebrated the Equinoxes. However, they are important points in the yearly cycle and some ancient monuments such as the holed stone at Men-an-tol on Penwith Moor in Cornwall were oriented toward the Spring Equinox rising Sun. Originally, the Celts were an inland people but the timing of the Equinoxes would have become obvious when they settled on the western coasts of Europe and fishing became a staple part of the economy. The Equinoxes are important to coastal peoples. They bring strong gales that are dangerous for fishing and high tides that are dangerous for those gathering shellfish. The latter can rush in and cut people off from the shore.

The Equinoxes are also important for settled agriculture. Spring Equinox is the time for sowing crops. Autumn Equinox is the time of the apple harvest when grain and fruit must be stored for the winter. Those reviving Celtic traditions have now brought the Equinoxes into the festival calendar. The revived Druid orders celebrate the Spring Equinox as Alban Eiler and Autumn as Alban Elued. In Wicca, Spring Equinox is Ostara and Autumn is Mabon.

FESTIVAL CELEBRATIONS

RECONNECTING WITH NATURE

Religion derives from the Latin word religare—to reconnect. Our aim in acknowledging the seasonal festivals is to reconnect ourselves with the wider cosmos. Reconnecting can take many forms. One of the most important ways to reconnect with the seasonal cycle is to observe what is happening in Nature. Time spent with Nature is healing. Experiences of solitude, silence, and greenness are an important part of Celtic spirituality. Life in polluted cities where we cannot see the horizon is unnatural for us and stressful. When rats live in overcrowded conditions, they attack one another. When humans feel overcrowded, we get neighbor-

*ABOVE **The Celts strove to attune themselves to the rhythms of nature. For coastal dwellers this meant that the strong gales which heralded the equinoxes could be anticipated and avoided.***

21

hood violence. To be alone with Nature, to listen to the noises of the wood, to have times of stillness and peace, all this enables us to hear the inner voice of the Divine. It gives us time to reflect on our daily life and on how we can live it more wisely and well.

ATTUNING TO
THE SEASONAL CYCLE

Before or on each festival go for a walk, ideally in the countryside or, if not, in a city park. Look at what is going on around you in Nature. Are the trees budding, in blossom, in full leaf, fruiting, covered with dead leaves, or bare? What are the birds doing, the animals, the flowers? Is it a time of growth and new life, of flowers and fertility? Is it a time of warm Earth and ripe crops? Or is it a time of decline and loss, of stillness and decay, or of the crisp refreshing coldness of winter?

Breathe the air; feel the Sun, wind, or rain upon your skin. Place your hands upon the Earth and feel the pulse of life within her. Place your hands on the trunk of a tree and feel its ener-

gy. Is its sap rising? Is it awake or sleeping until winter passes? In all these simple actions, you are using your senses to reconnect with Nature, which is the garment of the Divine.

ALTARS AND SHRINES

We go out into Nature and feel at one not only with Nature but with the Divine realm beyond. Then we get back into our vehicles and drive back into the city, losing that connection once more. How can we retain that peace and harmony and bring it into our homes and everyday lives?

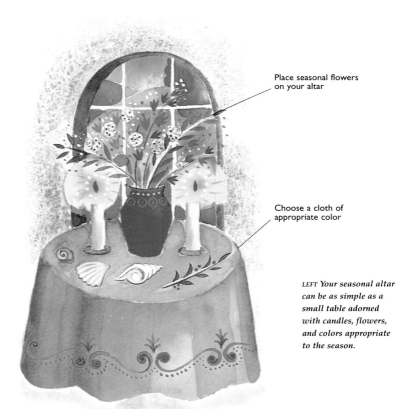

Place seasonal flowers on your altar

Choose a cloth of appropriate color

LEFT Your seasonal altar can be as simple as a small table adorned with candles, flowers, and colors appropriate to the season.

As a starting point, why not dedicate a particular place in your home as a small sanctuary, shrine, or altar? This could be a shelf or a small table. Cover it with a cloth of a color appropriate to the season. Here are some color suggestions:

FESTIVAL COLOURS

Samhain • brown, black

Midwinter • red, green, gold

Imbolc • white, pale green

Spring Equinox • green, yellow

Beltane • green, white, pink

Midsummer • gold, rose

Lughnasadh • orange, gold

Autumn Equinox • orange, brown, red

Find or buy some flowers, plants, or seasonal greenery to put on your altar. Add some other symbols of the season. You could have candles of an appropriate color and any other objects that feel sacred to you. You might like to add the statue of a deity, or some beautiful natural object that you have found—a rock, seashell, crystal, a piece of twisted branch.

Your altar need not look pious to an outsider. A table covered with a cloth, flowers, and candles is a beautiful and yet welcoming sight in your home. You need not have any deity symbol, and to a stranger your simple altar may be simply home decoration; but for you it can represent something more.

SACRED SPACE

Why, might you ask, do we need an altar when the Divine is all around us? An altar is a focal point for the sacred and for the spiritual powers that guide us through the universe. Our minds are lazy. An altar helps remind us of the sacredness of our everyday world and of the Divine and our relationship to it. Creating an altar can be a meditative and devotional act in itself. In traditional societies, people spent hours of their time creating beautiful objects to please the gods.

It is important in our consumer-oriented culture to take time to focus on the nonmaterial realm.

*ABOVE **Nature provides an abundance of beautiful ornaments with which you can decorate your home. Seashells can make an attractive alternative to flowers.***

Often modern life teaches us to concentrate on what we do not have. Our cars are never new enough; our clothes are never fashionable enough. We must desire, consume and seek bigger and better things. This is not necessarily harmful. It is good to have ambitions and to strive to better our lives. It is also important to stop and take stock and to enjoy what we have already achieved. It is important to pause now and then and to ask ourselves what we are seeking and why. Often we are so busy doing that we take no time to reflect, digest, and plan our next step.

PAUSING THE
TURNING WHEEL

Quiet periods of reflection are when we halt the turning wheel for a moment. We let time stand still. We tell our friends not to call, we put the children to bed, switch off the television, and put on the answer machine. We turn off our electric lights and see the world for a time by the glow of candlelight and flickering shadow and flame.

In this darker world, there are gateways of the imagination that lead us to the Otherworld of myth and delight. Our unconscious minds can send messages to us in these quiet times that tell us our true needs. These may differ from the conscious wishes

LEFT Clear space and time for a quiet moment of reflection and listen to your inner voice.

Light candles to meditate by

and ambitions that we hold. We hear the voice of unease as we pursue a goal that is not truly fulfilling. We hear the small plea within ourselves for outlets for our creativity, something we may have neglected in the frenzy of everyday living. We hear the tiredness of our bodies and learn when to give them rest. In quietness, silence, and tranquillity, our inner psyche finds its voice.

DAILY OBSERVANCE

Once you have an altar, you have a small point of stillness in your home and a focus for meditation. Many of us are shy about formal prayer. Yet often we send out small spontaneous thoughts to the Divine.

Perhaps each evening you could go to your altar and spend five minutes in meditation. You could light a candle and speak to the Divine of your needs. You could send out loving thoughts and healing to others. The energy of the universe is one of balance. As we ask, so we give. As we give, so we receive. A conversation with the Divine can be simple. It can be a short prayer to God, or to Goddess if for you the Divine is more female than male, in which we give thanks for the gifts that we have received and ask for guidance in the coming day.

Gracious spirit in whom we live and move
  and have our being,
thank you for the help and guidance you have
  given me this day.
I ask you to guide me in the day to come.
Show me what it is you would have me do,
  and grant me the strength and courage to
  do it wisely and well.
So mote it be.

REMEMBERING

It is also important to remember the needs of others in our requests. This is not because we want to earn merit points in the life hereafter, or because we want to think ourselves virtuous. Remembering others is an act of love that gives great joy to the giver.

When we have finished, we can be silent for a moment and then put out our candle. By these small steps, we build our spiritual links not only to the Divine, but to all those who enter our thoughts at such times.

Often we make pleas for Divine assistance—and then forget completely that the cosmos has heard and answered us! Before you make your requests to the Divine, take a small piece of card or paper and write down your requests. Leave it hidden somewhere on or under your altar where no one can see. When it is time to change your altar cloth for the next season, read your requests to see if there have been any changes in your situation. Then burn your requests in a candle flame. Maybe the Divine will have heard you, maybe not; but it is important to ask, to speak our need. The universe does listen, even if our requests cannot be answered exactly how and when we wish.

Seal your note and keep it hidden

*ABOVE **Articulate your needs or requests to the Divine by writing them down – this will also help you see at the end of the season whether any have been answered.***

RITUAL

Communing with Nature, making a seasonal altar and beginning to form a relationship to the Divine are ways to start to live in harmony with and to honor the cycles of Nature. Later you might to create some simple ceremonies to celebrate the festivals.

The ancient myths and rituals that are the cultural treasure house of our ancestors contain truths about the development of the human race. Many would say that they represent metaphysical realities: that they are dramatic representations of the interplay of the Gods, the Divine forces of the universe. However, it is not necessary to believe this in order to find value in seasonal ritual. The rites are not only a way of contacting the Divine outside us, but also a way of understanding our inner psyche and contacting the Divine within. Each festival has a deep psychological meaning and, by integrating these celebrations into our lives, we can come to understand our innermost being.

CELEBRATIONS

Many of us feel that ritual is an empty show: it is not for us. Ritual can be pompous, wordy, boring, and authoritarian; a chance for a priest to talk down to a fidgeting congregation. Our seasonal rituals can be very different. They can show us the meaning of our lives and how we as individuals fit into a greater whole. They can speak through a symbolic language that allows us to come to an understanding of those processes of life and death which are our lot. We learn to praise and honor the Divine which nourishes and cares for us.

Seasonal rituals are enjoyable. Too often we surround spirituality with piety and a sense that living a spiritual life is about self-denial when it should be about joy. A ritual is a celebration of the joy of being alive. Human beings are extraordinary creatures. We are animal bodies with conscious minds, matter imbued with spirit. We live in a world of wondrous beauty and to have awareness that enables us to experience this world is an incredible gift. Living is not easy and consciousness is not with pain. Our seasonal festivals can help remind us that even in the darkest time there is the hope of dawn, that after illness comes recovery and that after death is rebirth.

LOOKING AHEAD

Through this book, we shall learn of the Celtic festivals, their history, and folk customs. For each festival, there are simple ceremonies that we can perform alone or with family and friends. We will learn the importance of celebrating the sacred in our everyday lives. We will learn why the festivals are meaningful to us today. Together we will learn how to attune ourselves to the cycles of Nature and the ever-turning wheel of life, death, and rebirth. We will reconnect to the cosmos and so become part of a universal whole that is greater than our individual selves.

For we are the children of Earth

and of the starry Heavens,

and there is no part of us.

that is not of the Gods.

BELOW Communing with nature can take the form of simply being outside, where all the senses can be awakened to the changing beauty of the landscape.

SAMHAIN

In this darkest, coldest, bleakest season, Samhain marked the onset of winter. It was a time of death, when the earth lay bare and livestock were slaughtered for the long winter ahead. The veil between this world and the Otherworld was lifted, and the spirits of the dead rejoined the community in the feasting and celebrations. Bonfires were lit on hilltops for purification and symbolized the longed-for regeneration of the life-giving Sun.

OPPOSITE *Hallowe'en is a modern festival in which many vestiges of the ancient festival of Samhain are evident.*

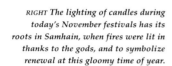

RIGHT *The lighting of candles during today's November festivals has its roots in Samhain, when fires were lit in thanks to the gods, and to symbolize renewal at this gloomy time of year.*

In Ireland, and in many other Celtic countries, the festival of **Samhain** (pronounced Sow'in) was the beginning of the New Year. Samhain means Summer's End. In most of the Northern hemisphere, by the beginning of November summer has truly ended. The nights grow long. It is often dark before we leave work or college. As we go home, the roads and pavements are strewn with fallen leaves. The trees strip themselves of the greenery they cannot support through the winter. Throughout winter, they will sleep and stand bare and skeletal against the dark sky.

DEATH AND BEYOND

The New Year in all traditions is a time of celebration. For the Celts, it was a time to gather around a warm fire in the chieftain's hall; to drink and to eat freshly slaughtered meat. It was a time for warriors to sheathe their swords and to boast of their exploits, while bards wove tales of their deeds and valor.

Samhain is also a Festival of the Dead. Our Celtic ancestors knew that Samhain brought death. Winter brought snow and frost. No animals could graze. They had to feed on hay stored from the summer fields. Only a few animals could be fed through the winter. The rest were slaughtered and their meat salted. With the cold, the elders of the village were vulnerable to illness. The death rate would go up with the onset of November; something that is still true today.

The season of Samhain is a natural time to think about death and to remember those who have gone before. Many European countries honor their war dead on November 11, the date when the First World War ended. In Catholic countries, November 1 is the first of two days for commemorating the dead. The first is **All Saints** which honors those who have been united with the Divine in heaven. The second is **All Souls** which commemorates those who have not yet reached heaven but are in a place of spiritual purification which Catholics call *Purgatory*.

OVERCOMING FEAR

For New Year to be a Festival of the Dead may seem strange to the modern mind. We hide death away. It has become something fearful. Earlier generations saw dead bodies from an early age. It was the custom in my father's part of Ireland to hold a wake—a party to celebrate someone who had died. The dead person was an honored guest—laid out in an

open coffin or, in some cases, propped up in the corner in his or her favorite chair.

I now make my home in Brittany, the Celtic northwestern corner of France. Until the 1950s in traditional villages, the dead were buried under the church floors. The bodies were dug up again

ABOVE **Samhain was a time for honoring and commemorating the dead, and for heroes and warriors to be remembered in both tale-telling and song.**

31

once the flesh had fallen from the bones. The bones and skulls were then displayed in ossuaries—open-fronted bone depositories of carved stone. These were by church entrances, so people could stop on the way into church and say a quick prayer in front of Grandma's thigh bone. This honoring of the bones of the dead is the same tradition that our Neolithic ancestors followed 5,000–8,000 years ago. Death and the dead were constantly present and were treated with less fear.

Samhain is the time of transition from one year to the next. It is a time for coming to terms with death; something which many of us find difficult. Samhain takes place during the astrological sign of Scorpio which is a Water sign and strongly associated with the sea. Water transforms and changes, washing away pain and sadness and cleanses wounds. Scorpio is ruled by the planet Pluto, named after the God of death and

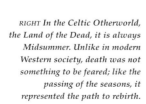

RIGHT *In the Celtic Otherworld, the Land of the Dead, it is always Midsummer. Unlike in modern Western society, death was not something to be feared; like the passing of the seasons, it represented the path to rebirth.*

the underworld in Roman religion. Before that, in Greece, his name was Hades and to the Celts, he was Dis. At Samhain, we honor the power of death. This takes away life but grants release from pain and suffering and entry to the Otherworld.

TIR NA N'OG

Our Celtic ancestors believed that when they died they went to the Otherworld. This was also known as **Tir na N'Og**, the Land of Youth or the Summerland. Irish myth tells the beautiful story of Etain who reincarnates as the wife of Eochy, High King of Ireland. Her previous husband who dwells in the Otherworld comes back to find her and appeals to her to leave Ireland (ERIN) and return

with him to Tir na N'Og. He uses symbolism from Nature to hint at the loveliness of the Land of the Dead which is a place of hope, and beauty.

Celtic spirituality teaches reincarnation—that we do not live once, but many times. In Celtic tradition, wisdom cannot be attained in one brief lifetime and the Wheel of Rebirth will turn many times before our journey ends.

Reincarnation is often thought of as an Eastern teaching, but this is not the case. The Druids taught of the transmigration of souls—that after death the soul would incarnate again. What we decide about reincarnation is for us alone, but it is important to remember that prior to Christianity the doctrine of reincarnation was the most widely accepted belief about the afterlife. Traces of this are found in the myths of all European peoples and in early Christianity. There may have been many more references to reincarnation that were suppressed by later unsympathetic recorders of Pagan myths.

THE PLEA TO ETAIN

O fair-haired woman will you come
    with me
to the marvellous land, full of music,
where hair is primrose yellow
and skin whiter than snow?
There none speaks of "mine" or "thine"—
white are teeth and black are brows;
eyes flash with many-colored lights,
and the hue of the foxglove is on
every cheek.
Pleasant to the eyes are the meadows
    of Erin,
but they are as a desert to Tir na N'Og.
Heady is the ale of Erin,
but the ale of Tir na N'Og is headier.

It is one of the wonders of that land
    that youth does not age.
Smooth and sweet are the streams that
    flow through it;
mead and wine abound of every kind.

◆

O lady, if thou wilt come to my
    strong people,
the purest of gold shall be on thy head—
thy meat shall be pork unsalted,
new milk and mead shalt thou drink with
    me there,
O fair-haired woman.

Traditional Irish

HALLOWE'EN AND SAMHAIN

Many modern Hallowe'en customs come from ancient Samhain celebrations. "Trick or treating" is part of the celebratory side of Samhain. At the transition between one year and the next, the normal laws and conventions do not apply. Children had licence to do as they pleased and could go around the houses of the village demanding "favors" or else!

Another Samhain custom is the making of Jack O'Lanterns—pumpkins carved into grinning heads with lights inside. Our Celtic ancestors revered the head, which they saw as the seat of inspiration and learning. In battle, heads of worthy opponents were cut off and taken back to display in the communal hall. This may seem barbaric to us today, but our ancestors' lives were harsher and rawer than our own and they did not share our physical squeamishness.

Some Samhain customs involve apples. The apple was considered a mysterious fruit that had something about it of the Otherworld. In many European mythologies, eating the golden apples of the Goddess gave eternal youth. "Aval" or "Afal" in Welsh and Breton means apple. The *Avalon* of Celtic Arthurian myth, where the dead King journeyed to await rebirth, is *Apple Isle*.

One traditional custom is bobbing or ducking for apples. We fill a large cauldron or pot with water and float apples in it. Each person must retrieve an apple from the cauldron using only his or her mouth. This is not as easy as it sounds. On one level this is a simple children's game. On another level is a deeper symbolism. To begin the New Year, each person must gain an apple, the symbol of life, to show that he or she will survive the year to come.

SAMHAIN CELEBRATIONS

CELEBRATION

Everyone loves Hallowe'en, so one way to celebrate is to give a party. We can invite friends and family; or we can party alone, enjoying our own space and company. Party decorations can include everything associated with Hallowe'en "witchiness" —bats, broomsticks, ghosts, and all. Make your Jack O'Lantern by hollowing out an orange pumpkin or two and carving a face—two eye holes, a hole for the nose, and a smiling mouth with teeth. The inside of the pumpkin can be kept to make pumpkin pie or pumpkin soup.

Other foods are those traditionally associated with this time of year: baked potatoes, pork, fruit cake. Any food that is solid and warming is appropriate for the onset of winter. Make a seasonal altar by decorating a small table with symbols of the season. Fallen leaves such as the beautiful red leaves of the maple tree are appropriate. You could also have pinecones and flowers such as chrysanthemums. In the center, place a large thick red candle.

HONORING THE DEAD

Parties are for the living, but at Samhain they are also for the dead. This is the season for honoring our ancestors. It is a good time to get out photograph albums and family trees and to tell stories of those who have gone before. As well as our seasonal altar, we can make an ancestors' altar with photographs, mementoes, medals, and small name cards. This altar should be lit with small votive lights such as those found in Catholic churches. It is customary to put some token food and drink on the altar—bread, pie or cake with apple cider. This is left out all night in case the ancestors should choose to come and eat.

RIGHT Shamans and druids would invoke their spirit guides by dressing up in masks and costumes, another example of a Samhain tradition which has filtered through into its modern counterpart, Hallowe'en.

We have physical ancestors. We also have spiritual ancestors; those whose dreams and visions inspire us. They are our own private list of "saints" and heroes, whose names we might like to add to our ancestors' altar. Perhaps they are spiritual teachers, perhaps those who have made great breakthroughs in medicine or those who have struggled bravely for freedom and peace

AFFIRMING LIFE

We can begin our party with bobbing for apples. Fill a large pot, bowl, or cauldron with water and float an apple for each person. Small ones are best. If you want the game to be easy, leave the stalks on. If you want a challenge, pull them off! Each person must retrieve an apple using only their mouth. Do not eat the apples until all are retrieved.

THE APPLE

As you cut the apple, say:

Behold the pentacle, the five-pointed star of Earth, Air, Fire, Water, and Spirit.

May we be blessed in body, mind, inspiration, feeling, and spirit,

this coming year and all those that

are to come.

Show the pentacle in the center of the apple to those around the table. Now pass it to each person in turn and give them the blessing of the year to come:

Blessings be for the year to come.

Each person should pass on the apple and the blessing to the next person around the table.

Cut apple horizontally to see the pentacle

RIGHT **The five-pointed star-shape in a cut apple is a natural representation of the pentacle—the ancient symbol of life.**

PUMPKIN PIE

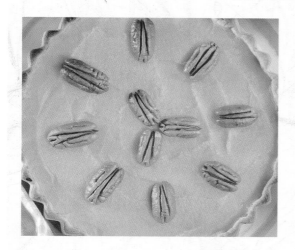

PASTRY

- 1 cup all-purpose flour
- Pinch salt
- 1/4 cup butter, margarine, or lard
- Cold milk

PIE FILLING

- 1lb cooked, mashed pumpkin
- 2 eggs
- 1 cup evaporated milk
- 1/2 cup brown sugar
- 1 tsp ground cinnamon
- 1/4 tsp ground allspice
- Pinch nutmeg
- Pecan halves for decoration

If you think you are allergic to nuts,
do not include them in the recipe

To prepare the pastry, sift the flour and a pinch of salt into a mixing bowl. Rub in the fat until the mixture resembles fine breadcrumbs. Stir in enough cold milk to bring the mixture together into a firm ball. Cover and chill for about 30 minutes before use.

Roll out the pastry on a lightly floured surface to a circle about 11 inches in diameter.

Wrap the pastry around a lightly floured rolling pin and lower it into a 10 inch round pie dish.

Press the pastry into the dish and flute the edge or crimp with a fork.

Prick the base lightly with the tines of a fork.

Combine all the filling ingredients in a mixing bowl and beat with an electric mixer until smooth. Alternatively, use a food processor. Pour into the pie crust and bake in a preheated 425°F oven.

Bake for 10 minutes at this temperature and then lower the temperature to 350°F and bake for a further 40–50 minutes, or until the filling is set. Decorate with a circle of pecan halves.

In Celtic myth, there are always polarities; for the message is one of eternal change and renewal. On the festival of the dead, we also affirm the power of life. Once everyone has his or her apple, one person can demonstrate the mystery through a "showing." In traditional custom, the tribal elders, shamans, or priesthood would demonstrate a complex idea in a simple, symbolic form. Lay one apple on a chopping board or plate and cut the apple horizontally. Inside is a five-pointed star, the pentacle, a traditional symbol of life. The points of the pentacle represent the four elements of material creation, Earth, Air, Fire, and Water, surmounted by the fifth nonmaterial element, that of Spirit. Hidden within the pentacle are seeds, from which new apple trees will spring. The ever-renewing powers of life are thus revealed.

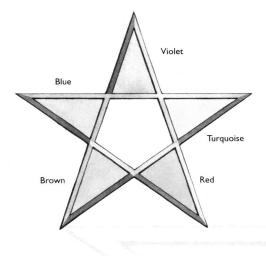

ABOVE *The Pentacle; the sign of life.*

not, you may have an open hearth where you can lay a fire. Otherwise, light the red candle on your seasonal altar for your Samhain fire.

In traditional societies, lighting fire is a matter of thought and ceremonial. Fire is honored as a magical gift from the Gods. Let the oldest person present light the Samhain flame with solemnity and a blessing for those present and for the year to come; for on Samhain night we honor the wisdom of age. Often when people die we have unfinished business—things we should have said and things we should not. One way of communing with dead friends and family is to write a letter and to send it to the Otherworld by burning it in the Samhain fire. Before celebrations begin in earnest, we can have a quiet and meditative time for those who have messages they wish to send.

SAMHAIN FIRE

After apples, it is a good time for fire. Lighting a fire is an important part of Samhain celebrations. If you can, have an outdoor bonfire and fireworks too. If

LOOKING TO THE FUTURE

Samhain is the time when the veil between this world and the Otherworld is thin. It is a traditional time for divination. One method is to color the cauldron water left from our apple bobbing with black ink. This makes a dark pool into which we can peer. If we have the sight, visions will come. Another Samhain divination is to peel an apple, keeping the peel in one continuous strand. Then throw the skin over your shoulder. The pattern in which it falls will show the first initial of the name of your lover in the year to come. You could also read the tarot. All these different methods are ways to see through the veil between present and future.

AFTER SAMHAIN EVE

The day after Samhain night has another traditional purpose. This is the day when we tend our ancestors' graves, if we have them. If not, why not take some flowers to the grave or memorial of some local person who has given their devotion to the community? We have our well-known national heroes, but why not do some research to discover our local and often unsung heroes too? The food and drink left from our ancestors' altar can be scattered here for the birds.

Autumnal colours of Samhaim

Fruit may be taken to adorn a grave

RIGHT **Samhain is also a Festival of the Dead, and a time to remember and pay respect to those who have gone before.**

WINTER SOLSTICE

On the shortest day and the longest night, with the Sun rising and setting at its most southerly point and its power at its lowest ebb, Winter Solstice celebrations and rituals marked the return of the lost Sun to the northern hemisphere and its victory over the darkness of winter. This was symbolically fused with tales of the birth of a Sun Child, or Divine Child, and was a time of great joy and feasting.

OPPOSITE *Winter Solstice celebrations have survived in the West in the form of Christmas, and central to this festival is the old Pagan symbol of life, the evergreen tree.*

In the black season of deep winter, a storm
    of waves
crashes along the edge of the world.
Sad are the birds of the meadow,
save for the ravens that feed on
    crimson blood.
At the clamor of harsh winter—
rough, black, dark, smoky—
dogs are vicious in cracking bones;
the iron pot is put on the fire
at the end of the dark black day.

Irish, attributed to Amergin, eleventh century

In the county of Meath northeast of Dublin, once the land of the High Kings of Ireland, stands the 5000-year-old Neolithic burial chamber of New Grange. It was built at about the same time as Britain's Stonehenge. Its stones are covered with the same beautiful spiral patterns as those on the Neolithic burial chambers of Brittany and Scotland.

The entrance to New Grange is in the southeast, the direction from which the sun rises at Winter Solstice. For 51 weeks of the year, the inner chambers of New Grange are in darkness. On the morning of Winter Solstice, a shaft of light strikes through the doorway illuminating the dark heart of the chamber of death. At this moment hope is reborn in the darkness.

Winter Solstice in the shortest day of the year—and the longest night. We know that light affects the psyche. Long hours of daylight stimulate the pituitary gland and help keep us in a positive and happy mood. Lack of light leads to sluggishness and depression. The more we stay indoors, the more likely we are to suffer from lethargy and "winter blues." To go out to meet the cold is important at Winter Solstice.

ABOVE The ancient Neolithic burial chamber at New Grange, built 3,000 BC, was constructed so that its internal passageway was oriented to catch the first shaft of light from the dawning Solstice Sun.

With Winter Solstice, the wheel of the year reaches its lowest point and shortest day, and then— the great miracle—the day grows just marginally longer. For our ancestors, Winter Solstice was a time for feasting. It was a time to enjoy goose or pig. Houses were decorated with greenery and bright red-berried holly. One of the biggest logs was burned to make a warm blaze. Women baked sweet honey cakes and bought treats for the children from passing peddlers—a brightly colored ribbon, a wooden toy. All these were ways to affirm hope in the dark time and to bring just a little color and joy into winter's cold and harshness.

ABOVE In December the Roman festival of Saturnalia celebrates the overthrow of the old god Saturn by the new, Jupiter, and heralds the triumph of spring over winter.

THE GOLDEN CHILD

Winter Solstice in many traditions celebrates the birth of the Sun Child, the Child of Promise, who will mature and become the young God of the Spring. Christianity absorbed these earlier myths into the story of Christ. Jesus was not necessarily born on December 25th : it is more likely that this date was adopted by Christianity because there were already Pagan traditions that celebrated the birth of a Divine Child on this date.

At Winter Solstice the Sun moves from the sign of Sagittarius, ruled by the planet Jupiter, to Capricorn ruled by Saturn. Jupiter rules royalty and kingship; Saturn is the way of the hermit. Saturn is concerned with buried treasure, the light hidden under the bushel. This is the path of the Sun Child who is born in obscurity. His Divine parentage is unknown until he reveals himself as the solar hero who is to defend us against the powers of evil.

There is a message here. We must judge each person on his or her merits and encourage each child to fulfil his or her potential. We are not all kings and heroes, but the message of the Winter Solstice Sun Child is that we each have a spark of

DECEMBER

JOHN LEIGHTON.

RIGHT The hero of Irish myth and legend, Cu Chulainn, was born at Winter Solstice time and this was celebrated as the birth of the Sun Child, who brought with him all the hope and promise of the New Year.

GIFTS AND COMMUNICATION

Winter Solstice is a time of celebration, giving, and rejoicing; for in the cold, dark days of winter, there is the promise of spring to come. Winter Solstice is about communication and community. In modern life, this is the time of seasonal greetings cards. In the dark time of the year, we remember with love our relatives and friends. Winter Solstice is also a time of gift giving and a time to show generosity of heart.

Our gift giving and card exchanging can become mechanical. We sign our names to a card and insert a copy of a word-processed circular letter. It is good to give a little more of ourselves. Take time to write a personal message in a card. It could be thanks for help and friendship, a reminder of some activity you shared or of something wise the person said that made you think. All these acknowledge that person's unique

the Divine golden fire within us. Each of us has a part to play in weaving the tapestry of the world. We can live our ordinary life like heroes if we bring to whatever we do—our work, our studies, our parenting—the best that we can give. However simple the task, we can bring to it the light and love of the Sun Child.

individuality, the Divine spark that makes him or her different to others. Acknowledging others in this way is a spiritual gift from them to us; something that can be much more important and meaningful than a gift bought in a store.

Winter Solstice is a season of peace and good will. Maybe there are people we have quarreled with during the year; things that were left unsaid, or times when we said too much. We cannot undo the past but, if we care about those we have hurt, this is the time to say sorry; to send a card or to pick the phone. To make the first move in a mutual quarrel can be difficult; but it is a sign of inner strength not of weakness. We may be rebuffed, but we can respect ourselves for trying, even if we do not succeed.

ABOVE To bring life, energy, and renewal into your home, decorate it with traditional seasonal greenery collected fresh from nature.

SEASONAL SYMBOLISM

Imagine you are walking through a forest of deciduous trees that stand bare and skeletal against the winter sky. Suddenly in the midst of the forest, you find a holly tree covered in rich, thick green leaves and smothered with red berries. All the birds of the wood are singing here and feasting on these fresh red delights. Imagine the leap of hope this would have given our ancestors in the winter days. What would be more natural than to cut a branch and to bring it home to decorate the house?

It is also traditional to bring home mistletoe. We tie a piece to the ceiling and anyone standing beneath it can claim a kiss from anyone else. Mistletoe was a sacred plant in Celtic tradition. Its white berries symbolize the energy of the sun. Another name for it is "All-heal." It was widely used in medicine and in the treatment of cancer. Its possibilities for cancer treatment are being investigated by pharmaceutical companies today.

Winter Solstice is also a time of flame and fire. If you are lucky enough to have an open fire or a stove, you can follow the traditional practice of going out to find a special log to burn on Winter Solstice night.

WINTER SOLSTICE CELEBRATIONS

CELEBRATION

The longest night usually begins on the evening of December 21 and finishes on the sunset of December 22. There can be slight variations in different years, but most diaries will tell you when the shortest day occurs. If you can, set aside a whole day for the seasonal celebration. You might want to celebrate the Solstice a day or two before or after the exact date if the Solstice is not on a weekend.

DECORATIONS

In the day leading up to the sunset beginning the Solstice, collect some seasonal greenery to decorate your home. If you can go out into the countryside to search the woods for your greenery so much the better; but you should know that our ancestors believed that trees were living beings and should be treated with respect. Do not cut more greenery than you need. Take a sharp knife and make a clean cut at an angle just above one of the nodules on the twig or branch. This nodule will produce new growth in the spring. Thank the tree and perhaps leave it a gift of a silver coin. Hide your coin in the earth beneath the tree and ask for a blessing on your home and family.

If you would like to have a decorated tree, try to find one that has roots and can be replanted. If you buy a small tree, you may be able to keep it outside in a pot and bring it in every year for Winter Solstice until it grows too large.

For your altar cloth and candles you need red and gold for warmth and Sun, and green for the evergreen world of Nature

Woods are a good place to search

Collect only the amount of greenery you need

ABOVE Although winter is a harsh time of year, outside you will find a wealth of leaves, berries, and twigs for your Winter Solstice altar.

and for the Mother Goddess who renews the Earth. You can add to your altar anything that reminds you of the Sun: golden apples, sparkling crystals, Sun symbols, golden candlesticks. Add some of your seasonal greenery—holly, mistletoe, and sweet-smelling pine branches. You will also need a golden candle for each person attending your celebration and a holder in which to place it when lit.

ABOVE The sun is paler and weaker at this time of year. In hope of its regeneration light candles in your home.

HOSPITALITY

To our Celtic ancestors hospitality was a sacred duty. In keeping with this tradition, you might like to invite others to celebrate the Solstice. In these times our friends may be from many faiths, or from no faith at all. A Solstice celebration can be a nondenominational way of bringing together friends of different beliefs. We may give our deities different names, or we may honor the Divine as nameless and beyond the confines of any creed. In simple celebration that invokes the archetypal forces of life, we can find our common ground.

EVENING

As sunset approaches, get everyone to take a shower and put on their best clothes. The solstice is a joyous time and it is good to dress up to greet it. As night falls, light the house with candles. Play some ancient music such as Irish harp music or medieval carols. Their sounds awaken deep ancestral memories within us. Winter Solstice was a time to drink warming drinks such as mulled wine. The Celts loved wine and imported vast amounts from southern Europe. Dried fruit and nuts still in their shells are good to nibble with our warming brew.

SONG

As we sip our drinks, we might want to make some

music of our own. If you have a musician in the family, all the better. If not, you could try singing. You can buy books of carols in any store that sells music. Not all carols are holy. Medieval carols were made to be sung from door to door and in the communal feasting hall. Often their words were too earthy for Church. Many carols may be older than Christianity and may have had Christian meaning grafted to them. In recent years attempts have been made to

rediscover the original words. Here are some words by Norman Iles who has attempted to restore many of the more preChristian sounding carols—or you may decide that you prefer the Christian version.

ABOVE Singing with family and friends can be a good focal point for Winter Solstice celebrations.

THE HOLLY AND THE IVY

All: The Holly and the Ivy

When they are both full grown

Of all the trees that are in the wood

The Holly bears the crown.

◆

Men: The Rising of the Sun

And the running of the deer

Women: The rounding of the Shining Moon

The weary, worn Hunter.

◆

Men: The Holly bears a berry

As red as any blood

Women: And ivy bears the greenest leaves

To wrap him in her hood.

◆

Men: The Rising of the Sun

And the running of the deer

Women: The rounding of the Shining Moon

The weary, worn Hunter.

Men: The Holly bears a prickle

As sharp as any thorn

Women: And ivy bears a clinging vine

To smother him right down.

◆

Men: The Rising of the Sun

And the running of the deer

Women: The rounding of the Shining Moon

The weary, worn Hunter.

◆

Men: The Holly bears a bark

As bitter as any gall

Women: And ivy bears small nectar flowers

To sweeten all his fall.

◆

All: The Holly and the Ivy

When they are both full grown

Of all the trees that are in the wood

The Holly bears the crown.

MULLED WINE

INGREDIENTS

to serve four

- 3 small oranges (or clementines or satsumas)
- 2 lemons
- bottle of red wine (or alternatively mead, red grape juice, or nonalcoholic wine)
- 3–4 tablespoons of brown sugar
- cloves
- cinnamon
- For those who do not drink alcohol, red grape juice or nonalcoholic wine can be used. You will need less brown sugar with these. Mead can also be substituted for the red wine.

Grate or cut the surface of the peel from the oranges and lemons. Do not include the white pith underneath. Clementines, satsumas or other small oranges that do not have thick pith are best.

Pour all the red wine into a pot.

Add a large cup of water.

Start to heat slowly.

Add brown sugar to taste. Try 3 or 4 tablespoons to start.

Add the peel. You can also add slices of orange and lemon if you wish.

Add cloves and cinnamon to taste.

Heat until the mixture simmers gently. Do not let it boil.

Serve in cups or mugs.

WISHING

Now is the time to light the candles on your Winter Solstice altar. We light candles to symbolize the return of light into our lives. Allocate a golden candle to each person. Light a taper and then put out the lights.

One by one, light your candles from the taper and make a wish. Let the youngest child start, probably with a little help from a parent. Our wishes can be silent or spoken aloud. On this occasion, they should be not for ourselves, but for someone else. Winter Solstice is a season for giving.

THE MOTHER

At Winter Solstice we celebrate not only the Sun Child, but also his Mother; she who brings new life and hope to the land. When everyone has made a wish, light a green candle for the Mother and say:

Queen of the moon, Queen of the sun,

Queen of the heavens, Queen of the stars,

bring to us the Child of Promise!

It is the Great Mother who gives

   birth to him;

it is the Lord of Life who is born again.

Darkness and tears shall be set aside,

when the Sun shall come up early.

Golden Sun of hill and mountain,

illumine the land,

illumine the world,

illumine the seas,

illumine the rivers;

grief be laid and joy be raised!

Blessed Be the Great Mother,

without beginning, without ending,

from everlasting to eternity!

Blessed Be!

GIFT GIVING

At Winter Solstice, we give but we can also receive. Ask each person who comes to your celebration to bring a gift. Give as a guideline a price that you know everyone can afford. Get everyone to sit back to back in a circle holding their gift. Play some music and pass the presents around behind your backs so no one can see what they have. When someone calls stop, each person keeps the present they have at the time.

What if you are celebrating alone? The same principles of giving and taking apply. Buy yourself a gift. Is there some music you would like, a piece of jewelry, a book? Buy your gift and then place it on your altar for your Winter Solstice celebration. Place three golden candles on your altar. Light these and make three wishes for others. Now take the gift that

LEFT *Display your Christmas gifts on your seasonal alter with lighted candles. Pause to reflect on the gifts and on the people with whom you are exchanging them.*

Take time to prepare and wrap your gifts

Make wishes for others by candlelight

Decorate the altar

you have prepared for yourself. While it is nice to have others give us gifts, one consolation of buying our own is that for once in our lives we get something exactly right!

FEASTING

Winter Solstice is a time for feasting. Decorate your table with red, gold, and green and dine by candle light. Pork was a traditional dish at this time. The Celts were also greater eaters of fowl. Chicken and turkey are familiar to us, but for something more

unusual, you might like to try duck. You will find recipes in most cookbooks.

Another alternative is salmon. This may be more acceptable if your guests are from faith communities with different dietary requirements. In Celtic tradition, the salmon was considered to bestow the gift of wisdom. You might also want to make a vegetarian nut roast for guests who do not eat meat or fish. You can find recipes in vegetarian cookbooks or you can buy nut roast ready-made from health food stores or other large food stores. Your nonvegetarian friends will usually enjoy helping eat it as well.

AFTER THE FEAST

Solstice morning is a good time to give something back to Nature. Birds are very important in Celtic tradition. There is beauty in their song but they were also seen as messengers between the Divine realm and that of Earth. This is a tough time for birds. If you have any leftover bread or cake from your feast, go outside to feed the birds. Each extra bit of food will help them survive.

This is a good opportunity for children to see birds close up and to learn their names. Often children today do not know the names of the other life forms that surround them. As human beings we share our planet with a whole community of living creatures and we need to learn how our actions affect them. Learning their names is a good starting point for children to begin to understand that the other sentient beings of the universe are important and are our friends.

*BELOW **Birds experience the hardship of winter first-hand. By feeding them you are helping them survive, and giving something back to Nature.***

Attracting birds to the garden provides a link with nature

Make sure food you put out is suitable for birds

IMBOLC

As the days lengthened and the Sun's warmth increased, the burgeoning of new life across the earth was marked by the festival Imbolc. Agricultural activity recommenced: the land was prepared for new crops; lambs were born and ewes began to lactate. The fertility of the land and the miracle of motherhood were central to the festival and were celebrated and honored through offerings to the archetypal goddess of womanhood, Brigid

OPPOSITE *To experience the hope and potential of Imbolc just look outside at the blooming of new life as flowers, new shoots, and blossom start to push through.*

Raw and cold is icy spring,

cold arises in the wind.

The ducks of the watery pool

    raise a cry,

passionately wailful is the harsh-

    shrieking crane which the wolves

    hear in the wilderness at

    the early rise of morning.

Birds awaken from the meadows;

    many are the wild creatures from

    which they flee,

out of the wood,

out of the green grass.

*Irish, attributed traditionally
to Amergin,* **eleventh century**

The feast of **Imbolc** marks the transition from winter to spring. Some believe that Imbolc or Oi-melc means "ewe's milk." Another idea is that the word means "in the belly." Imbolc begins at sunset on February 1 and ends at sunset on February 2. In temperate climates, Imbolc is when the first signs of spring appear. Winter is a time of rest. We shut our windows and turn up our heating systems until spring comes again. For our agricultural ancestors, one sign that the rigors of winter were ending was the beginning of the lambing season. Ewes would be pregnant at this time and nearing giving birth to their lambs. They would also be ready to produce milk. Sheep's milk was highly prized and was used to make delicious white cheese.

Another sign of Imbolc is the first green shoots appearing above the earth. Sometimes, as with snowdrops, the shoots come up through the snow itself. Imbolc is a hopeful time. Life is stirring again. The forces of creativity are beginning to wake. The

ABOVE *Imbolc is traditionally associated with
the beginning of the lambing season
and the birth of new life.*

days grow noticeably longer. We know that even if difficult times are still to come, new life is abroad in the land. Imbolc was the beginning of a season of reawakening for human beings. Agricultural activity began in earnest. It was time to plow the soil and prepare it for the next year's crop. Long nights would be spent outside helping the ewes with their lambing.

ABOVE *The celebration of motherhood is central to Imbolc, making it essentially a women's festival.*

BRIGID, BRIDE

In preChristian Celtic tradition, Imbolc was sacred to the Goddess Brigid who was also known as Bride (pronounced Breed) and Brigantia. In the Celtic Church, she became a saint and Imbolc was celebrated as St. Brigid's or St. Bride's day. Brigid was a patroness of the learning, poetry, prophecy, healing, and of the craft of the blacksmith. She was also patroness of virgins. A woman on her wedding day —the Bride—is her representative. In the Christian era, Brigid or Bride was believed to have been the Virgin Mary's midwife and was invoked to help women in childbirth. In Scotland, Christ was known by the beautiful title of *Dalta Bride bith nam beannachd,* the foster-son of Bride of the Blessings.

Imbolc in the Christian calendar was also *Candlemas*, the feast of candles and the *Purification of the Virgin Mary.* In Jewish tradition, child birth was considered polluting. Before mothers could attend the temple again, they had to be purified. When Mary went to the temple to be purified after the birth of Jesus, it was Brigid who walked before her bearing a lighted candle.

The *Carmina Gaedelica* is a collection of Scottish Gaelic prayers translated by the nineteenth-century folklorist Alexander Carmichael. In *Geneaology of Bride*, we find many prayers to Celtic saints that were originally addressed to Celtic deities. *Geneaology of Bride* is part of a prayer to Bride to protect her worshipers from harm.

Every day and every night,
that I say the genealogy of Bride,
I shall not be killed, I shall not
be wounded ...
no fire, no sun, no moon shall burn me,
no lake, no water, nor sea
shall drown me.

Excerpt from GENEAOLOGY OF BRIDE

LEFT Ancient worship of the mother-goddess was carried through into the Christian faith in the worship of the virgin mother, Mary.

the Church of the Oak. A fence surrounded the fire which no man was permitted to cross. When Ireland became Christian, Brigid's holy fire became the responsibility of nuns. The monk Gerald of Wales wrote of how 19 nuns guarded the fire, taking turns to keep vigil. On the twentieth night the nuns slept and Brigid guarded it herself. The nuns continued to tend the sacred flame until the thirteenth century, when the Papal envoy Henry of London ordered the nuns to extinguish it. The local population was furious and forced the Bishop to have it relit. Brigid's sanctuary was finally closed on the orders of the English King Henry VIII during his Protestant Reformation.

BRIDE IS WELCOME

In nineteenth-century Scotland and Ireland, young unmarried women made a special doll at Imbolc from some of the previous year's wheat. The Bride doll was dressed and decorated with shells, crystals, and any first flowers. The girls then formed a procession and took Bride to every house in the village singing a song to her. Afterward there was a feast. Young men came to pay Bride homage. Celebration and dancing continued until dawn

SACRED FLAME

In Ireland, the chief shrine of Brigid was at Kildare. It was an ancient custom to honor deities by burning a perpetual flame at their shrines. This custom continues in Catholicism where a flame burns in front of church altars. In Ireland in the Pagan era, a group of unmarried priestesses known as *Inghean an Dagha*, Daughters of Fire, tended Brigid's flame. The fire was in a holy settlement by a sacred oak tree that was later renamed *Kildare*—

when the girls sang a final song to Bride. Older women made their own Bride doll and prepare a decorated bed for her in a basket. Bride was brought ceremonially into the house with the words, "Let Bride enter; Bride is welcome." The blessing of Bride on the house was requested for the coming year. The Bride doll was then laid in her bed so that she could sleep overnight in the house.

In Ireland, Bride's Cross or Bride's Star—a woven equal armed cross of rushes—was hung above the door to protect the house from harm and fire. The rushes must be pulled up rather than cut and must be woven deosil, from left to right, the direction of the sun's path across the sky. There are similar rush or straw charms in Native American tradition. Wool versions called *God-eyes* are made in Mexico.

VIRGIN MOTHER

Imbolc is above all a women's festival. Imbolc is associated with recovery after childbirth and with that phase of motherhood when children become more independent and mothers can have some

time to themselves again. Bride is a virgin goddess. In preChristian Celtic tradition, love-making was thought natural and not necessarily reserved for marriage. A virgin goddess was an unmarried goddess, not necessarily a nonsexual or a childless one. This is why, despite being a virgin goddess, Bride is also a midwife. Above all, Bride is a goddess of independent womanhood. For this reason, she has come to be a patroness of women's self-expression and creativity. For a man, she has come to be the muse who inspires his creativity.

PURITY AND HEALING

Water was important in Celtic religion. The landscape of the Celtic world, Ireland and Brittany in particular, is littered with healing springs and wells. Many are dedicated to Brigid or Bride, a patroness of medicine. Celtic medicine was advanced and in Brittany there was even a psychiatric hospital run by Druids near a sacred spring later dedicated to Merlin.

LEFT Seasonal flowering bulbs can provide an ideal decoration and a splash of color in your home at Imbolc.

Imbolc takes places when the Sun is in Aquarius. Aquarius is the waterbearer and brings us the cleansing waters of life. Imbolc is a good time to check our health and to seek healing if we need it. Aquarius is also a sign of rationality and of seeking new knowledge. Ruling the modern science of psychology, the energy of Aquarius is pure and balanced, and it helps us find **Gnosis**—the saving knowledge of the Divine—which comes like a light in the darkness to illuminate the mind and spirit.

CHANGE

Imbolc is a season to rid ourselves of what is worn out. An ancient Irish tradition was that husbands and wives could leave one another at Imbolc. This custom persisted into the twelfth century, well after Ireland became Christian. We need not do anything as drastic; but if we are in a negative relationship, this is the time to change it.

Imbolc is a good time to examine our jobs, relationships, the way we spend our leisure time. Are we engaging in positive activities that enhance our well-being and self-esteem? If not, how can we change things? Imbolc is a time to plan new enterprises and to make the first moves toward bringing them into actuality.

ABOVE *Trees, so sacred to the Celts, are vital to the process of regeneration and renewal at this time of year, bringing healing to both the earth and the atmosphere.*

IMBOLC CELEBRATIONS

CELEBRATION

Imbolc is a time to clean our homes, clothes, and other possessions. At Imbolc, the Divine feminine, the Goddess, or in Catholic tradition, Bride the midwife of God, is welcomed into our homes. If we are to entertain a special guest, we want to prepare for her.

Cleansing can be a spiritual act in itself. One of the great teachings of the Christian monastic tradition was *Laborare est orare*— to work is to pray. If we perform simple actions with love and spiritual intent, they become something much more.

Salt is the great sterilizer and is used in spiritual cleansing. To cleanse your home not only of dirt but also of negative influences, dissolve a tiny amount salt in the water you use for cleaning. Avoid getting salted water on metal objects, though, because it will corrode them. Once you have got rid of negative energy, bring positive energy into the home. Smell has a strong effect on our psyches. To bring a light and warm energy into the home, try polishing furniture not with polish containing synthetic chemical perfume but with that traditional monastic product —beeswax polish.

COMMUNING WITH NATURE

Once we have prepared our-selves and our homes, how can we celebrate Imbolc? Go outside to the countryside or to a park to commune with the world of Nature. What signs of new life are

Traditional beeswax produces the best shine

Salt is a spiritual cleanser

SALT

BEESWAX

Nourish wood by polishing

*LEFT **Make spring-cleaning part of the purification rites of Imbolc. Try to use natural, chemical-free products such as beeswax polish and salted water.***

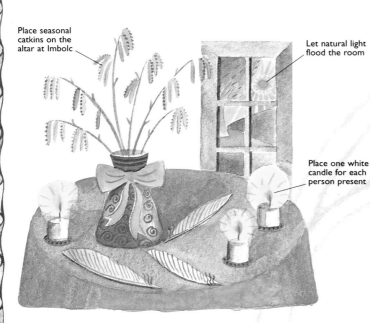

Place seasonal catkins on the altar at Imbolc

Let natural light flood the room

Place one white candle for each person present

RIGHT Although natural decorations may be sparse at this time of year, your altar can still be made beautiful with the simplest of objects, such as feathers, and the creative use of color.

emerging with the lengthening days? How does the energy of the world feel to you? As you walk the earth—or perhaps even the snow—sense the ground beneath your feet. It is home to myriad life forms whose lives nourish the soil, which in turn gives us our food. The bodies of all species decay back into the Earth and so renew her again. We are all part of the endless cycle of life.

ALTAR

In these early months of the year, there may be little to bring home from the outside world for your altar, but perhaps a beautifully shaped twig, early catkins,

or a feather may catch your eye. Pots of flowering bulbs are an ideal decoration. You can grow bulbs yourself over the preceding months or you can buy them from a store. Snowdrops with their pure whiteness and bright green leaves capture the essence and meaning of Imbolc perfectly.

The altar cloth should be pale green or white. On the altar, you will need a white candle for each person present and a candlestick in which to carry it. Alternatively, you could use small votive lights in their own containers. Candle magic is traditional at this time. If you would like to do candle magic for a personal intention, you will need to choose an appropriate color. Orange is good for seeking a new job, green for seeking new love, gold for health, white for purification, and violet to develop psychic powers. Blue is good for recovery after psychological illness and red if you need energy and physical strength. Pink brings peace and calm. You will also need some oil to anoint the candle. An aromatherapy oil is suitable or pure olive oil.

PREPARATION

Imbolc is a festival of purification. If you can, purify your body by taking a sauna or steam bath and cleansing the skin of winter's grime. Alternatively, purify your bath water by dissolving a small amount of salt in it. Now change into clean clothes, to welcome the energy of Imbolc into your home.

A RITE

Imbolc is a meditative time of the year. You may want to have friends and family around you, or you may wish to celebrate alone, but either way the energy should be calm, quiet, and contemplative.

First, light your altar candles, but leave any candles for candle magic until later. Put out the lights, take a candle each and go to your front door and open it. Your candle flames are to welcome the energy of Imbolc into your home. If you are celebrating with friends, you might like to make an image of Bride to bring through the doorway. In this case, one person should wait outside with the image until the door opens. Otherwise simply visualize the energy of the Divine feminine, whether as goddess or saint, coming into your home like a gentle cleansing breeze. Each person can say out loud, or silently if you prefer:

THE DIVINE FEMININE

Let Bride enter.

Bride is welcome.

Bride is come.

Blessed be Bride!

Then bow to honor the sacred presence entering your home.

Set your front door wide open

Welcome Bride with candles

*ABOVE **Bring the energy of the Divine feminine into your home by welcoming the spirit of Bride through your front door.***

Celebrate with friends and family

Return to your altar and put down your lighted candles. Sit by your altar and contemplate the wondrous mystery of change and renewal that the season has brought with it. When you feel ready, you could address the goddess Bride in some way. Write your own prayer or use words like these:

GRACIOUS LADY

O Gracious Bride,
who walks between the worlds,
bringing light and life to women and men;
come forth once more and walk in
our ways.
For where you have walked
will spring forth flowers,
where you have smiled,
the Sun will turn and linger,
where you have sung,
the birds will return.
Gracious Lady, bless our homes,
may there be peace therein;
bless our bodies,
may they be well and strong;
bless our hearts,
may they know joy and love;
bless our minds,
may they know the delight of creativity;
bless our spirits,
may they know the ecstasy of the Divine.

ABOVE Candle divination can be carried out by dropping candlewax onto a bowl of water and interpreting the random patterns it forms.

CANDLE MAGIC

It is now time for any candle magic you would like to perform. Let each person take their candle and visualize what they are seeking. Your visualization should show the event as having happened. If your candle magic is for health, visualize yourself well, healthy, and walking around again. If your candle magic is to get a job, visualize opening a letter that tells you that you have the job. If you are seeking a new relationship, visualize walking hand in hand with someone and being very happy.

As you hold your candle in your hands, visualize your intent. Hold the image in your mind for as long as you can. Now take your oil and put a small amount on your fingers. Oil is a substance that carries spiritual energy. Anoint the candle. Start in the middle and smooth the oil toward each end of the candle. while focusing on the visual image of your wish being fulfilled. Avoid getting the oil on the wick of the candle—it will make it splutter. Use a candle that is already burning on your altar to light your new candle. Place in its candlestick. Now ask the Divine realm to bless your magical intent. You can use your own words for this, saying what is in your heart, or you can say something like this:

> Gracious Bride, bless this my intent and
>
> bring it to birth on the Earthly plane.
>
> So mote it be!
>
> After the candle has burned for a period, put
>
> it out saying:
>
> As I extinguish this flame on the
>
> earthly plane,
>
> may it burn more brightly in the realm
>
> of spirit.
>
> So mote it be

Usually magical candles are burnt bit by bit over a period such as a week. If you start on a Sunday, burn the candle in roughly equal amounts each day finishing the next Sunday. Each time you light and extinguish your candle, say the same words as before.

Plant a tree with care, secure it with a stake

ABOVE *Trees play a vital role in sustaining the delicate balance of the atmosphere. Help maintain this by planting a tree yourself.*

HEALING THE EARTH

Another way of celebrating Imbolc is to plant a tree. Why trees? Imbolc is a season of healing and by planting trees we can help heal the Earth. Trees breathe in carbon dioxide and breathe out oxygen. They help regenerate the air that we breathe. As deforestation affects our planet, our atmosphere is steadily deteriorating. By planting trees, we can each do our part in helping the power of Bride to renew the Earth.

SPRING EQUINOX

With equal amounts of day and night over the earth, the Spring Equinox celebrated this rare balance in nature, and the triumph of the Sun over winter. It was the time of year when seeds were sown, and all the potential of life was held in the earth. Fertility and procreation were celebrated, and a feast in honor of the goddess Ostara, later to become Easter, hoped to ensure the fulfillment of the promise held by the land and the Sun.

OPPOSITE *The goddess Ostara was symbolized by the egg,* . *and this has remained a part of modern Easter celebrations.*

Light yellow primrose on the banks,

how delicate, bright, and fair your face;

as you grow entwined in clusters,

soft and shining, neat, spreading.

You are the hardiest bloom which comes from
   the earth;

you are decked out in Spring,

while the others still hide their eyes.

Scottish, Alexander Macdonald,
eighteenth century

ABOVE *The Spring Equinox heralds
the miracle of new life as seeds and
blossoms begin to push through.*

Spring Equinox is known as Alban Eiler in modern Druidry. This is a turning in the year, when the hours of daylight grow longer than the hours of darkness. By Spring Equinox we know that the seasons are really changing and that the life force is renewing. Birds sing and build nests. Trees open their pale-green buds. Day grows longer than night. Lengthening days bring new growth. The sap rises in the tree. The sexual urge awakens in the animal world and in our own.

If you go out into Nature at springtime, everywhere you will see greenness. New leaves are on the trees; grass is growing. All around us is the freshness of new life. Many spring flowers will be the yellow of the Sun. A beautiful flower of spring is the primrose, with its gentle yellow petals. It is best not to pick this since it withers too quickly, but to decorate your home you could buy pots of primroses or grow them from seed.

In many parts of the Celtic world, spring is the season of daffodils—blazes of golden yellow signal that the Sun grows stronger. Sometimes in Brittany, along the roof ridges of the thatched cottages people plant daffodils which bloom around Spring Equinox. Little houses with daffodils growing out of their heads look rather crazy, but it's a true sign that spring has come.

Eggs and seeds

Spring customs have been woven into the Christian festival of Easter. The word Easter derives from the German Goddess Ostara, whose name comes from the same root as the female hormone estrogen. Ostara's symbol is an egg. In some countries, eggs appear at Easter as chocolate eggs; in others, hard-boiled eggs are dyed green, symbolic of spring fertility. In Ireland children held races, rolling their hard-boiled eggs down hills to see whose was the fastest.

In gardening and agricultural calendars, spring is the time to sow seeds. It is also a common time of mating for birds and animals. Longer hours of daylight stimulate hormones that awaken sexual desire. In humans this happens through the stimulation of the pituitary gland, which is intimately connected with our hormonal cycles. The sap rises in the trees and in humankind too.

Courtship

Spring Equinox is a time of courtship. It is the time of conception of solar heroes. The Catholic Church celebrates the Annunciation of the Virgin Mary at this time. This is when she conceived the Christ

ABOVE The color yellow is associated with this time of year, as a blaze of yellow flowers covers the countryside.

child through Divine intervention. The great Celtic hero King Arthur was conceived at Spring Equinox and born at Midwinter Solstice. His conception was surrounded with love and magic.

Legends tell us that Arthur's father King Uther Pendragon fell in love with Igraine, wife of the Duke of Cornwall whose home was at Tintagel Castle on Cornwall's jagged northern coast. Uther's adviser, the magician Merlin, summoned a mist from the sea and in the foggy darkness, Uther entered Tintagel disguised as Igraine's husband. Uther gained entry to Igraine's bed chamber and Arthur was conceived from an adulterous union. It is Arthur's and his wife Guinevere's own sexual indiscretions that later destroy his kingdom. It seems that political leaders caused the same scandals and made the same mistakes then as now.

BALANCED CONDUCT

In the Northern hemisphere, Spring Equinox occurs when the Sun goes into the astrological sign of Aries, which is a Fire sign. Impetuous Ariens leap in feet first and then wonder how they got there. The urge of spring is to act. This is a valuable energy and we need it in our lives, but we also need to treat it with caution, balance, and common sense.

The ancient Celts believed that our actions would only be right and true if we lived balanced, harmonious, and virtuous lives. This would bring harmony to the land and prosperity and good fortune would follow.

The teachings of King Cormac, a third-century Irish king, represent the Celtic ideal of right and balanced conduct. From an early age, Cormac displayed such great wisdom that the Irish considered him to be the essence of truth. In the *Tecosca an Righ* or *Instructions of King Cormac mac Airt* he describes to his grandson Cairbre how he behaved as a young prince.

LEFT Stained-glass imges of Arthur, Joseph of Arimathea, and St. Michael are ranged together in this nineteenth-century church window.

I was a listener in the woods,

I was a gazer at the stars,

I was blind where secrets were concerned,

I was silent in a wilderness,

I was talkative among many,

I was good tempered in the mead-hall,

I was stern in battle,

I was ready to watch,

I was gentle in friendship,

I was a physician to the sick,

I was kind toward the powerless,

I was firm toward the powerful,

I was never harsh, lest I be satirized,

I was not feeble, lest I be humiliated,

I was not clinging, lest I should be
     burdensome,

I was not arrogant, though I was wise,

I was not given to promising, though
     I was strong,

I was not impetuous, though I was swift,

I did not deride the old, though
     I was young,

I was not boastful, though I was a
good fighter,

I would not speak about people behind
     their backs,

I would not reproach, but I would praise,

I would not ask, but I would give;
     for it is through these habits
that the young become old and
     kingly warriors.

ABOVE *Spring is a time associated with courtship, fertility, and conception, as represented by the feminine deity of the Moon goddess.*

71

THE WAY OF HARMONY

While none of us is a king or a queen, we can still practice the virtues of the Celtic nobility. At Imbolc we cleaned our homes and reviewed our lives. Spring Equinox is the time to take stock again. Have we done anything about the aspects of our lives that we found wanting at Imbolc? If not, now the Sun is in Aries, it is time to act and to set out to achieve what we planned. Spring is also the time to review our lives in another way.

This time we should look not at what we do but how we do it. In our love relationships, in how we interact with others at work, in our parenting, do we behave in ways that will bring harmony? Do we

listen to others, but also give of ourselves? Do we respect ourselves so that others do not ride roughshod over us? Do we give others respect? Where we see wrongdoing, do we have the courage to speak out or do we turn a blind eye? In our relationships, do we dominate others without letting them develop their own ideas and express themselves?

To think about these things we need time and silence. One of the best ways to give ourselves space and to clear the mind is to go on a minipilgrimage.

COMMUNING WITH NATURE

We may think of pilgrimages as a Christian tradition, but the urge to visit sacred places is part of all cultures and faiths. A good way to prepare for Spring Equinox is to spend the day outside and, if you can, to visit a sacred or special place. This might be a temple or church. It might be a special place in Nature, one that has been considered holy for centuries or one which is special for you. The mountains, lakes, seas, islands, caves, and canyons of our planet have all been revered by the ancients as places where the human world and the Divine can draw closer, communicate and merge as one. To visit such places gives us renewed energy and at the same time inner peace.

When visiting a sacred place, it is important to walk part of the way. In ancient traditions, walking was a meditative act. Our ancestors would walk to special places. They would also walk around specific sacred space such as mazes or, in the Christian monastic tradition, the cloisters. Mazes in particular allow people to make symbolic journeys that involve walking long distances but without leaving their homes.

We can make our minipilgrimage alone or we can ask friends and family to come with us. It is important to set aside part of the time for silent walking, but if you have small children this might be more like five minutes than fifty. This silent time is when we can think about our lives and whether our behavior reflects the harmony of the natural world. When you return from your walk, write down your thoughts about balance within your life and where it is lacking. Then, with the Sun in Aries, it is time to do something about it.

LEFT *The Celtic landscape, such as Killarney in County Kerry, shown here, has borne witness to centuries of human existence, and holds the memories of our Celtic forebears.*

SPRING EQUINOX CELEBRATIONS

CELEBRATION

If you are celebrating with others, arrange your altar so that people can stand around it in a circle. Cover your altar with a green cloth and decorate it with yellow flowers and budding twigs cut carefully from the trees. Take your piece of paper or card where you have written your thoughts about what imbalances you feel are in your life and hide it somewhere either on or beneath your Spring Equinox altar.

For your altar, you will need five candles of equal height with candleholders. You need a blue candle to represent the element of Air, red for Fire, blue-green for Water, brown for Earth, and violet for the fifth element of Spirit. In the Western Mystery Tradition, Air is associated with the east, Fire with the south, Water with the west, Earth with the north, and Spirit with the center. Together the five elements represent all of creation held inbalance.

You will also need some gold ribbon or cord. Cut the ribbon or cord so that you can lay out on the altar a circle with an equal armed cross at the center. This is the solar cross of Celtic tradition.

At the center of your cross, place the violet candle of Spirit. At the eastern point, place the blue candle of Air. At the south, place the red candle of Fire; at the west the blue-green Water candle, and at the north your candle of Earth. To work out where the directions are check in the daytime where the sun is in the sky. At noon it will be in the south, in the early morning it will be in the east, and just before sunset it will be in the west.

Your candles and solar cross represent the universe held in balance. This is the energy which you wish to bring into your life at this time. Balance

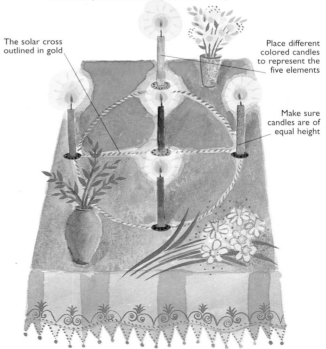

BELOW Different colored candles placed at the cardinal points on your Spring Equinox altar represent all the elements of the universe in perfect harmony.

The solar cross outlined in gold

Place different colored candles to represent the five elements

Make sure candles are of equal height

and energy may seem strange companions, but the teaching that energy comes from balance and harmony is found in all the arts from martial arts through to dance. Inner harmony produces an energy and creativity that is very different from that of a forced energy motivated solely by the will. It is an energy that is found when we work with the forces of the universe and the cosmic tides.

By working with a symbol such as the circle cross, we bring the energy of the symbol into our lives. This s the ancient philosophy behind sympathetic magic. Today, we might call this "sympathetic psychology," instead of magic. By working with ancient symbols we activate archetypal patterns of activity within our psyches. Symbols set energies in motion in the unconscious. These energies can then manifest themselves within our lives.

A SPRING RITE

An important part of the symbolism of springtime is seed sowing. You can do this indoors in pots of soil, or outside if you have land where you can plant seeds. If you want to celebrate with friends, ask people to bring a pot of soil. Everybody can then sow some seeds and take their pot home with them. Sowing seeds creates new beginnings and at springtime we can sow seeds that are infused with a wish for the months to come.

*ABOVE **The balance and energy that we see all around us in nature should be cultivated within us at this time of year.***

Make an invocation by candlelight

Choose seeds that are easy to grow

RIGHT **To invoke and celebrate the energies of creation and new beginnings, plant seeds in small containers and display them on your altar.**

First voice: **I am the queen of every hive.**
Light Air Candle

Second voice: **I am the blaze on every hill.**
Light Fire Candle

Third voice: **I am the womb of every holt.**
Light Water Candle

Fourth voice: **I am the shield of every head.**
Light Earth Candle

Fifth voice: **I am the tomb of every hope.**
Light no Candle

Sixth voice: **I am the chamber of rebirth.**
Light Sprit Candle

Seventh voice: **Thus it is made, the quatered circle of creation**
Extinguish Taper

We can wish that any enterprise we are beginning will grow strong and fruitful as the seeds grow. We could sow our seeds for a new relationship to come into our lives. Spring magic can be love magic. It can also be magic to conceive a child. Choose seeds that are easy to grow. We want to give our intention every help we can!

Before you sow your seeds, invoke the energies of creation. Take a taper and light your candles in the order of the invocation below. If you are celebrating alone, you can light all the candles yourself. If you have others with you, allocate a phrase to each person before you begin the rite and ask them to memorize it.

Stand in a circle around the altar, and pass the lighted taper to them before they say their phrase.

If you are with others, hold hands in a circle around the altar. You might like to say a litany of praise to the Great Mother who conceives the Sun Child at Spring Equinox and bears him at Winter Solstice. One person could say this, or a number of people could say a line each; if possible memorizing their line before the rite.

PRAYER OF PRAISE TO THE GODDESS

Blessed be the Great Mother,

Without beginning and without ending,

Blessed be her temple of pure white marble,

Blessed be the stillness of her holy place.

Blessed be the babe who cries to her,

Blessed be the deer who lift their heads for her,

Blessed be the birds who fly the skies for her,

(continued on opposite page)

Blessed be the trees which shake and sigh

    for her,

Blessed be the leaf that falls for her

and nourishes the soil.

Blessed be the wave which caresses the

    shore for her,

Blessed be the sand which succumbs to

    its embrace,

Blessed be the shell that is cast up from her,

Blessed be She, the Mother of Pearl.

Blessed be the stars which shine like jewels for

    her,

Blessed be the Moon in which we see her face,

Blessed be my spirit which soars the heights

    for her,

Blessed be my body, the temple of her being.

SEED SOWING

Now take your seeds outside or, if you are planting them indoors, let each peron take a pot of soil and some seeds. Hold the seeds in your hands for a while and focus on a magical intent—something you would like to bring to birth in the coming months. Then sow your seeds carefully in the earth and say a blessing.

Let us sow the seeds of life,

that shall bring forth new hope,

    new deeds;

and even as these shoots spring forth

    and grow to greenness,

so may new hope be manifest within

    our souls.

Keep the seed package so you can see how to care for your seeds.

Seed sowing is a piece of sympathetic magic. On a psychological level and on a magical level, by watering, potting out, and protecting our young seedlings, we are reminded constantly of the wish that we made with their planting.

Eggs are traditional at this time. These can be hard-boiled eggs dyed green with food coloring, but most people will enjoy the other seasonal variety—chocolate eggs—rather more. End your celebration by sharing a chocolate egg. Break the egg onto a large plate and pass it around with a blessing:

The blessings of the Lady to you,

    prosperity and good fortune!

BELTANE

As the hours of daylight increased and the high point of Midsummer approached, the Celts celebrated the festival of Beltane. This was a fire festival, where the disease and death of Winter were purged through the lighting of bonfires. Thoughts also turned at this time of year to the need to produce future generations to tend the land, and many aspects of this festival were associated with courtship and fertility.

OPPOSITE *At Beltane the earth is a mass of color and new life.*

Beltane, season supreme,

wondrous is its color then.

Blackbirds sing a full song

at the slightest light of day.

◆

The busy cuckoo calls aloud,

"Welcome splendid Summer!"

The bitter bad weather is past;

branches are thick with leaves.

◆

Burdened down with blossom,

the tiny bees

carry on their feet a mighty burden.

Cattle go up to their summer grazing;

the ant eats his fill.

◆

Delightful is the season's splendor;

the rough winds of winter are past.

Every wood shines white with blossom,

a joyous peace is summer.

Irish, Finn's Poem on Beltane
seventh century

Beltane means "bright fire" and this festival was sacred to the solar deity Bel or Belenos. The Celts venerated light and Sun and St. Patrick often likened Christ to the "true Sun." An eight-spoked Sun wheel appeared often on ancient Celtic altars. In Druidry and Celtic Wicca, it is a symbol of the Sun's journey through the Wheel of the Year, the seasonal festivals. In the Christian era, solar crosses were placed over graves and represented the resurrection into a new day.

ABOVE *The circular Celtic cross fuses the Christian cross with the symbol for the Celtic solar deity. This example stands at Monasterboice.*

A FIRE FESTIVAL

Many Celtic festivals involved fire, which was thought to have been brought from the Sun by a sacred bird—a swallow, wren, or swift. The red markings and forked tail of the swallow were the result of scorching by the Sun's rays. Part of Midwinter celebrations in Ireland was the hunting and capturing of a wren, the bringer of the Sun.

Fire was an element of purification. At Beltane, the Irish put out all their hearth fires. Great bonfires were built on every hilltop and the greatest of these was at Tara, the seat of the High Kings. In the darkness of night, the Druids kindled the flames at Tara. When people watching on the surrounding hills saw the glow of Tara's fire against the sky, they lit their own Beltane fires. Other watchers would see these flames and light their hilltop fires. In a short space of time, fires would be kindled all over Ireland. Once the fires were alight they were divided in two and cattle driven between the flames. This would protect them from disease by smoking parasites out of their hides which had snuggled there through the cold winter. When Patrick wanted to challenge the power of Ireland's Druids, he performed the sacrilege of lighting his fire before that of the High King at Tara.

To leap the bonfire was to take the flame inside yourself. The flame of light, life, and Sun would bring new life. Couples who wanted to conceive would leap the Beltane fire. They would also be helped by the lengthening days and sunshine that stimulate the pituitary gland and sexuality—as of course Nature intended.

The custom of making a new fire at Beltane continued into the nineteenth century in the Highlands of Scotland. Another custom was to make the Sun dance. This image appears often in Celtic poetry. This involved reflecting the Sun's light through an open window onto a bowl of water then shaking the water so that as it rippled sunlight danced around the room. To see the dancing of the Sun bestowed blessings on those who beheld it.

ABOVE For the Celts, Beltane was a fire festival, when fires were lit for luck, purification, and in honor of the fire and Sun deities.

TO GO A-MAYING

Traditional May Day rites have strong fertility associations. This remnant of the Pagan past found no favor with churchmen, Protestant or Catholic. In Britain, young men and women went into the woods on May Eve in order to gather blossoms and greenery to decorate their houses—or so they said. "And," Puritans noted disapprovingly, "many would emerge no longer maids." Similarly, the eighteenth-century Irish clergy condemned May Day festivities and "levity" at wakes, another traditionally social occasion in the rural calendar.

Rural life was much earthier than today. Often the bedding would precede the wedding. This was not only because young men and women are moved by the same impulses as today. Farming families needed many children to labor on the farms and to support their parents in old age. The work needed many hands and the more children they had, the more there were to work. Marriage often followed evidence of pregnancy.

OPPOSITE Dancing around the Maypole represents the infinite cycle of nature, with the dancing going first clockwise (sunwise) for life, and then counterclockwise (widdershins) for death.

ABOVE RIGHT The hilltop fires lit by the Celts at Beltane formed part of the purification rites, where the death and disease of winter was shaken off.

MAY QUEEN AND GREEN MAN

Traditional May celebrations involved crowning a May Queen, a young woman of childbearing age, who would parade through the village as a symbol of the young goddess of fertility. In Catholic countries there are sometimes similar processions today, but the young woman appears under a different guise—that of the Virgin Mary.

The Pagan god of fertility appears at May Day in the guise of Jack-in-the-Green or the Green Man, the consort of the May Queen. In British country customs, the Green Man was disguised by his garment of leaves and in the freedom of anonymity could do what he willed.

ARTHURIAN MYTH

The Green Man makes an appearance in the early Arthurian legends. The version of the Arthur story that is familiar to us today from the movies has undergone many evolutions. In early Europe, there were many different versions of the stories. It was only in Medieval Europe when the stories were written down that a rationalized and Christianized version was produced. This removed many of the original Pagan elements from the ancient figure.

Arthur was said in Welsh tradition to have had three wives. All three were called Gwenhwyvar, which is the Welsh form of Guinevere. Since all three wives had the same name, they may have been the same person but in triple form. In other words, it could be argued that Arthur was symbolically married to the Triple Goddess of the land.

In Celtic tradition, one of the Goddess' symbols is the horse. The Goddess appears in Welsh tradition as Rhiannon, the rider of the white mare, in Ireland as Macha, and on continental Europe as Epona. An image of the Goddess appears on coins as a naked woman with a spear and a shield riding a horse. This is an important reminder that in Celtic tradition women as well as men might be warriors.

GUINEVERE

Celtic noblewomen frequently challenged men to prove themselves worthy of their love by requesting them to perform daring feats of arms, rescue treasures, or fight wild beasts. In a Welsh version of the Arthurian legend, Gwenhwyvar challenges Arthur, who is not yet king, to prove himself to her by fighting a powerful warrior.

Gwenhwyvar the golden-haired challenges the dark-haired Arthur to prove himself. In folksong, taking the male steed to the women's well of water is often a sexual image. Gwenhwyvar's words may be a sexual challenge as well as a challenge of fighting prowess.

RIGHT In Celtic tradition the domain of warriors was not exclusively masculine, and there were many fierce women warriors.

Arthur:	**Black is my steed and bears me well, nor will he the water shun, and from no man will he retreat**
Gwenhwyvar:	**Bright is my steed of nature's hue: may the boaster always be despised. Only a real man is as good as his word. Who will rise and will be firm? Who will march in the front of battle? None but a hero can defeat tall Cai, Sevin's son.**

After their marriage, Gwenhwyvar tires of Arthur. We know of her love for Lancelot but she has earlier amorous adventures. On May Day when King Arthur is at war, she goes with her maids a-Maying in the greenwood. Melwas, a Scottish prince who was her lover before Arthur, hides himself in the wood dressed in green leaves, as the Green Man. Melwas frightens away Gwenhwyvar's maids who mistake him for the God of the forest and Melwas runs away with her to Scotland. In later texts, she appears as a virtuous Christian woman who is taken against her will. In the earlier text, she goes willingly.

BELTANE CELEBRATIONS

CELEBRATION

Beltane, like Samhain, is one of two great divisions of the Celtic Year. Samhain is for indoor night-time parties. Beltane is for outdoor daytime parties. You may have a yard or garden where you can celebrate. Alternatively, you could camp somewhere where you can party and light a Beltane fire.

Use pliers to cut and bend wire

Use fresh flowers

Twist flower stems to wire circlet

Ribbon to cover wire

ABOVE **Wear a homemade flower crown on May Day, using freshly cut flowers and leaves.**

If you are celebrating at home, begin the day by going outside to see what is happening in the world of Nature around you. Collect or buy blossoms and flowers to decorate your altar. Hawthorn blossom, also known as May blossom, is the traditional decoration for the house at Beltane. There are many superstitions about May blossom. Only witches could bring it into the house with impunity, my mother told me. However, on May Eve the taboo is lifted and anyone can do so.

WHAT TO WEAR?

If you can celebrate with family or friends, suggest everyone wears some form of Celtic or traditional dress. This is the time for women and girls to wear long flowing dresses and flowery crowns and to celebrate the beauty of womanhood. A long dress and a flower crown can transform the most elderly or least attractive of us to someone much more alluring than our everyday selves.

Flower crowns can be made by forming a circle of flexible wire just a little larger than your head. Fix flowers to your circlet of wire by twisting their stalks around the wire. Secure them by twisting short lengths of wire around them. Disguise the wire with ribbon. Instead of dressing up at home, ask people to bring their party clothes and flowers with them. Collect the women together to dress and to help one another make crowns.

The men can congregate for their own dressing up and to prepare a fire, barbecue and/or Maypole. It is traditional for men to have a crown of green leaves but some men's efforts look more like army camouflage than the headdresses of romantic Celtic chieftains. Women may prefer to take charge of the male crown-making themselves.

MAYPOLES

Circle dancing around a bonfire or decorated tree or Maypole dancing is traditional at this time of year. In Maypole dancing, ribbons are woven around a wooden pole. Men and women hold alternate ribbons. The couples face one another. Women dance sunwise, clockwise or deosil. Men dance counterclockwise, tuaithbel, or widdershins. The sunwise direction is associated with life and the tuaithbel direction with death. The men pass their ribbons over the first woman they meet and under the second. Women dance under the first man's ribbon and over the second. If everyone gets this right, a beautiful woven pattern appears down the Maypole. It is quite easy, but you have to concentrate. Once all the ribbon is used up, the Maypole can be danced undone and danced again. But be warned—it is much easier to weave the ribbons than to unweave them! The Maypole dance involves sunwise movement, the direction of life, and counter-sunwise movement, the direction of death. It interweaves the forces of creation and destruction, recognizing that death is the inevitable outcome of life and that after death, life is renewed.

If you would like to try Maypole dancing, for a party of about twelve you will need a wooden pole or cut tree about five or six inches thick and about nine feet in height. Straight fast-growing trees, such as birch or pine, are often used as Maypoles. You can dig a hole which will hold the tree upright, or you could have a slightly shorter and lighter pole and ask some strong guests to sit at the base and hold it. You will need an assortment of lengths of brightly colored ribbon about twelve feet long. You must fix these securely to the top of the pole. A staple gun can be particularly useful here. To accompany your dance, play some Irish or other folk music.

OTHER DANCES

You may know someone who can teach you some simple circle dances. If not, try dancing to some music that has three or four beats. Join hands and let everyone take three or four steps to the left. Then take three or four steps inward and the same number of steps back. Then take three or four steps to the left again. You will find that you are now performing a reasonably graceful deosil circuit. Perhaps you could add a few hand movements. As you dance inward toward the center, raise your hands. As you dance outward and to the side, lower them again.

Another simple dance is a chain dance. People stand in pairs facing one another so that half dance clockwise and half counterclockwise. First people join their right hands to their partners right elbow, then they pass behind one another, letting go arms as they do so. This will bring them facing a new partner. They take their new partner's left elbow, pass behind one another, letting go, and then take the right elbow of their third partner, and so on. Try putting music to a May chant and sing while you dance.

RIGHT As the sun sets on May Day, light a fire in the ancient tradition, in celebration and honor of its power and energy on which all life depends.

O do not tell the priest of our plight,

for he would call it a sin;

but we shall be down in the woods

all night,

a-conjuring Summer in.

And we bring you good news by word

    of mouth

for woman, cattle, and corn;

for the Sun is coming up from the South,

with oak and ash and thorn.

With oak and ash and thorn, my dears,

with oak and ash and thorn.

For the Sun is coming up from the South,

with oak and ash and thorn.

*Repeat until hoarse, tired, or your neighbors
have had enough!*

BELTANE FIRE

Just after sunset in the evening darkness is the time to light a Beltane fire. If you are not able to build a fire, then place your altar so that people can stand around it and light a thick yellow candle to represent the Sun.

In traditional societies, fire was considered a magical gift from the Gods. Fire lighting was conducted with reverence and ceremony. Choose someone to be your Fire Guardian to light the fire and keep a watchful eye on it.

Have everyone stand around the fire or candle and ask the Fire Guardian or another person to say the words of blessing. You might like to ask someone to learn the blessing by heart. Remember that the Celtic tradition is an oral one. This is based on a Scots Gaelic blessing.

Wear a
flower crown

Bless the Beltane
fire after sunset

LEFT The blessing of the Beltane fire, by whoever your group has chosen to be Fire Guardian, should be done orally in true Celtic tradition.

We kindle this fire today in the presence

of us all,

without malice, without jealousy,

without envy,

without fear of aught beneath the Sun,

but the High Gods.

Thee we invoke, O Light of Life,

be thou a bright flame before us,

be thou a guiding star above us,

be thou a smooth path beneath us.

Kindle thou in our hearts today,

a flame of love for our friends,

for our foes, for our neighbors all,

for all those upon the broad Earth,

from the lowliest thing that liveth,

To the Name that is highest of all.

ABOVE *Allow the natural romance of this time of year into your life and set aside time to spend with your partner, soaking up the beauty of the landscape together.*

FEASTING

Beltane is a good time for barbecues. You can barbecue all the traditional foods and you may want to provide some vegeburgers or vegetarian sausages for nonmeat-eating friends. Beltane is also a time for trying out wines made from the previous season's fruit and other crops. Your health-food store may have some country wines such as the beautiful and aromatic elderflower. Some stores also stock nonalcoholic elderflower drink. Mead would also have been traditional at this time.

SEXUALITY AND SENSUALITY

Beltane takes place when the Sun is in the astrological sign of Taurus, a sign of sensuality and material enjoyment, ruled by the planet Venus. The warm days of summer are a time to enjoy our bodies and our physical well-being. Beltane is a time of relationships and a good time to renew sensuality in our lives. If we have been with a partner for some time, and particularly if we have small children, it is easy to forget how to enjoy one another's bodies.

The day or evening after your May Day celebration is a time to rekindle romanticism. If you can, send the children off to visit grandparents or friends for the day. Beltane is a good time to renew your vows of love to your partner and to set aside time to be together. Spend some time in the countryside or enjoy a special meal. Give one another a massage and indulge in some leisurely sex.

If you do not have a partner, then take the opportunity to pamper yourself. Book a massage, steam bath, or a trip to the beauty salon. Enjoy having your body looked after.

Focusing on the body may seem a surprising way to finish a sacred festival, but it is important to remember that for our ancestors there was no divide between Nature and spirituality. Our bodies were gifts from the Gods and we should acknowledge their gift by enjoying our physical incarnation and the joyous world of the senses.

GIFTS TO THE ELEMENTS

Traditionally May crowns are given to the elements. They can be thrown off a cliff or high place where they can be borne away on the wind. They can be hung from a tree branch. They can be thrown on running water or burned in the Beltane fire at the end of your celebration. The message is that what has been taken from Nature must be given back.

LEFT **Reconnect with your sensual, physical self by pampering your body with luxuries.**

Indulge yourself with your favorite beauty products

Pamper yourself by candlelight

SUMMER SOLSTICE

With Solar energy at its most potent, it is not sur-prising that the Celts celebrated the longest day of the year by honoring the Sun and its associated deities. With the Earth in full flower, and the night short and bright, celebrations took place outside and involved feast-ing, playing games, and the lighting of bonfires, as well as the observance of the dawning of the Solstice Sun.

OPPOSITE *Summer Solstice fires are still lit in many parts of the world, such as this one in Bergen harbor in Norway.*

A good season is summer for long journeys;

quiet is the tall fine wood,

which the whistle of the wind will not stir;

green is the plumage of the sheltering wood;

eddies swirl in the stream;

good is the warmth in the turf.

Irish, attributed to Amergin, eleventh century

Summer Solstice or **Alban Arthuan** is the Longest Day in the Northern hemisphere when we honor the warming powers of the Sun that bring life to the land. Often in Western mythology we think of Sun gods and Earth goddesses. In Celtic myth we find both Sun gods such as Belenos and Sun goddesses such as the Irish Grania and Áine, and the Breton Belisama.

The Irish lit bonfires on Summer Solstice Eve to welcome the Sun. Flaming bundles of hay or straw were carried into the fields and among the cattle to bless them. In Limerick a fire was lit on the hill of Cnoc Áine by the village of Knockainy. At the end of the nineteenth century, the Goddess Áine was said to have appeared to a group of girls on the hill. She told them

to hurry with their celebrations because the fairy folk were waiting for the humans to go home so that they could have the hill to themselves.

Summer Solstice bonfires were opportunities for young men to prove their courage, strength, and agility by leaping the flames. Once the flames had died down, young girls who wanted to marry early and have many children would follow. Leaping the flames was thought to encourage the Sun to shine throughout the summer and to bring a good harvest. In some parts of Brittany, the Maypole stood until Summer Solstice Eve when it was cut down to form the Summer Solstice fire.

Summer Solstice was also a time of festivals at sacred wells. In the Christian era, wells were placed under the patronage of a saint, such as the famous St. Patrick's well in County Down, Northern Ireland. The pattern or pardon, the spiritual part of the day's celebration, involved religious services and drinking the sacred waters for healing. The evening involved another type of drinking; not to forget other activities beloved of the Celts—dancing, fiddling, courting, gambling, and fighting.

DECLINE AND DANGER

It is at Summer Solstice that the Sun is at the height of its power. However, that which reaches its peak is then at the point of decline. From Summer Solstice, the days will begin to grower shorter.

Summer Solstice was a transition point and therefore a time of danger. Rites of protection were common at Summer Solstice. An Irish custom to protect against disease was for the oldest woman in the town to recite prayers while going three times deosil around the Summer Solstice fire on her

knees. People raced home with burning hazel sticks from the fire. The first person to take a stick over the threshold would be blessed with good fortune in the coming year.

OPPOSITE **This statue is a depiction of Summer, and one of the group of four statues representing the seasons, found in the vineyards of Chateau Rivière, Fronsac, France.**

RIGHT **In Arthurian legend, the marriage of Arthur and Guinevere not only represents the joining of masculine and feminine, but is also symbolic of the union between the goddess of the land and the holder of power on earth.**

THE SACRED MARRIAGE

Summer Solstice is a festival associated with kingship. It was Celtic custom for kings to be married symbolically to the goddess of their tribe, who represented sovereignty. The relationship between goddesses of the land and the holder of worldly power—the king—is an important theme in Celtic mythology. This relates to ancient ideas of family inheritance. Originally this was matrilinear—passed through the mother's descendants. Land would be passed down the female line and, to become king, a warrior would marry a royal princess. This may have been why the Egyptian Pharaohs married their sisters. Many fairy tales tell of the exploits of young heroes who, by demonstrating their bravery, quick-wittedness, fidelity, and their favor with the Divine, win the hand of a princess and become king.

ARTHUR

The relationship between the masculine and the feminine is hidden in the symbolism of Summer Solstice. The Sun King is in the height of his powers in the Northern Hemisphere when the sun is in the astrological sign of Cancer, ruled by the Moon and the most feminine sign of the Zodiac. The true solar king is therefore one who knows and honors the feminine within himself and within others.

King Arthur was a solar hero born at the Midwinter Solstice. He fought for the powers of light and right against the forces of destruction and darkness, but he was a warrior in the service of his people rather than a fighter for fighting's sake. He fought in the service of the feminine. There were three major women in his life, symbolic of the Triple Goddess. Morgan, the fairy woman, whose name means the **Woman of the Sea**, was his half-sister. Like the sisters of the ancient Pharaohs, she was both his sister and the mother of his child. Gwenhwyfar or Guinevere was his barren wife. Viviane, the mysterious Lady of the Lake, was his guardian. It was she who entrusted to Arthur the sword of justice, **Excalibur**. It was returned to her care when it was time for the dying King to cross to the Island of Avalon to await rebirth.

TRUTH

The king's marriage with the land meant that he and the land became one. It was essential that he remain in good physical health or the land would fail. It was also essential that he be in good spiritual health. For this he must be truthful and of high integrity.

Truth is a serious matter because at stake is our integrity—that which makes us whole and what we

We are told of King Cormac mac Airt:

It was well with Ireland in the time of that King:

it was not possible to drink the waters of her rivers,

on account of the spawn of her fish;

it was not possible to travel her forests easily,

on account of the amount of their fruit;

it was not easy to travel her plains,

on account of her flowers and bees making honey;

all of which had been granted him from Heaven,

through the truth of his princedom.

are. In the *Acallam na Senórach*, the *Colloquy of the Ancients,* St. Patrick asks Caoilte mac Ronan what are the qualities most valued by the Pagan Irish. Caoilte's answer is "truth in their hearts, strength in their arms, and fulfilment in their tongues." These ideals still hold good today. It is a pity that more of our leaders do not aspire to them.

OPPOSITE *Stonehenge, Wiltshire, England, where the ancient stones are aligned to capture the first ray of the dawning Solstice sun.*

SUMMER SOLSTICE CELEBRATIONS

CELEBRATIONS

Summer Solstice is a celebration of the height of summer and of solar energy and healing. For your seasonal altar, you will need a bright-colored altar cloth—gold or rose is appropriate. Decorate your altar with anything that reminds you of the Sun—golden candlesticks and candles, sun symbols—and bright summer flowers, such as roses. A Summer Solstice altar should be one that makes you feel happy when you look at it.

Summer Solstice is a good time to spend some days outdoors, perhaps camping or hiking. This may mean that you will need to celebrate on a weekend and your Summer Solstice celebration could be a few days adrift from June 21 to 22. This does not matter. Ancient festivals frequently took place over five or more days. If your celebration is a few days either side of the "official" date, that is not a problem.

VIGILS

Many sacred sites, such as Britain's Stonehenge, were aligned to allow the Sun's light at Summer Solstice dawn to strike them. People would gather to keep vigil all night to watch the event take place.

If you are able to camp or to light a fire in your yard, then you can keep the ancient tradition of Summer Solstice being a night of watchfulness. Keeping a long night vigil is a good preparation for

ABOVE Solstice fires can be a good focal point for your summer celebrations, and an ideal place to keep warm during your all-night vigil.

Spend the night story-telling or singing

Light a good fire in celebration

any major changes or transitions we are planning to make in our lives. Young men who were about to be knighted kept such vigils over their weapons. If you are with friends, you can take it in turns to keep watch while the others sleep.

STORYTELLING

Alternatively, you can spend the night talking and singing. Our ancestors were great storytellers and regaled one another with tales of the heroic past. You could ask people to read some Celtic myths and legends and to bring one tale, poem, or song of kingship or queenship to the vigil to tell to the rest.

See if you can persuade your guests to learn their story or poem. The Celtic tradition was an oral culture and our grandparents' generation knew many tales, poems, and songs by heart. In modern life we have forgotten the art of memory, but it is important to nourish our psyches with myths and legends that we can pass on to others. A positive point if your guests have to learn their contributions is that they are unlikely to go on for too long! It also avoids the difficulty of trying to read by flashlight.

PERSONAL STORIES

Another form of storytelling is to ask everyone to tell the story of their lives. Unless we enter therapy we rarely tell the whole story of ourselves as we truly see it. The idea may seem strange at first, but try asking everyone to tell of their childhood, adolescence, early twenties, and beyond; speaking of their joys and sorrows, their achievements and disappointments at each phase. With a large number of people, you could divide into small groups so that everyone has a chance to speak. The darkness is a time of intimacy and people will discuss many things by the light of star, Moon, and fire, that they would feel inhibited about in daylight.

You might like to have a separate men's group and women's group for this and to separate husbands and wives. If people know each other better though, it can be valuable for one sex to hear of the joys, struggles, hopes, and fears of the other.

Women may find this easier than men. Our culture still teaches men to be reticent about their feelings. However, as an encouragement to men, it is important to remember that Celtic culture did not see manhood in the same way as the Anglo-Saxon culture that is so dominant in the West. If you read Celtic myth and legend, you will see that Celtic heroes are expressive. They adorn themselves; they weep and cry; they speak their feelings. And they are brave, good lovers, fight for their homelands, and do all the other things that a warrior must do.

DAWN

As dawn rises, wake everyone up or conclude the storytelling. It is time to give thanks to the powers of the Sun that bring life, healing, light, energy, and joy. You could stand and raise your hands to the Sun and say:

Arise, Oh Sun, let the darkness of night
fade in the beams of thy glorious light.
Send us strength and wisdom in the name of
    the Divine.
Ancient ones of the past we salute you;
generations yet unborn we send you greeting.
Hail to the Sun in the morning of the
world! Hail!

*Encourage each person to say something in praise
of the Sun, then bless a goblet of golden wine.*
Blessed be this Cup,
made in the image of the Holy Grail, the Cup
    of the Wine of Life that brings healing and
    blessedness to all who drink.
Blessed be.

Salute the Sun as you take a sip of wine:
Hail to thee, O Sun of Suns,
light of life and healing power.

*As the Sun rises above horizon, sit or kneel down
and place your palms on the Earth.*
Blessed be the Earth, Mother of us All.
We proclaim that there is nothing
    within Nature
which is not a reflection of the love of
    the Divine,

and within all creation is the evolution
to that which is better and best.
We salute the harmony of the cosmos and the
    beauty of Nature.
We find honor and humility, the seed
    of Peace;
in peace and in simplicity, the flower of love;
in love and in contentedness, the life
of joy;
in joy and in wisdom, the light of hope;
in hope and in nobility, the heart of goodness;
in goodness and virtue, the love Divine.

*Now bless a plate or basket of cake or bread, the
produce of the Earth:*
O Queen of Earth and Heaven
bless this food for our bodies,
and bestow upon us health, wealth, strength,
    and joy,
and the love of life
which is perpetual happiness.

Pass the cake or bread around with a greeting:
Blessings of Summer Solstice morn to you!

If you have kept vigil all night, you will need to sleep for a while. Then, before noon, try if you can to go to a place where there is clean running water. Take with you some small silver coins. Giving gifts to the spirits of the waters was an important tradition among the Celts. Tribes gave their finest jewelry, weapons, and furnishings to the Divine and asked a blessing in return. Summer Solstice is a good time to ask the Divine for healing for yourself or others. Take a clean coin for each person for whom you wish to make a request. As you make your request, cast the coin into the waters at the height of the noonday Sun.

Then salute the Sun once more.

Great One of Heaven, Power of the Sun,

we praise thee in thine ancient names—

Michael, Balin, Arthur, Lugh—

come again as of old unto this thy land.

Lift up thy shining spear of light to

protect us;

put to flight the powers of darkness;

bring us fair woodlands and green fields;

blossoming orchards and ripening corn;

bring us to stand upon the hill of vision;

and show to us the lovely realms of

the Gods.

Now find a shady spot for a picnic lunch.

a stream
er spirits

LEFT *Your all-night vigil will be rewarded by the sight of first ray of the returning sun, and the warmth of it on your skin.*

LUGHNASADH

The most important part of the agricultural year, the first harvest of crops, was marked by the festival Lughnasadh. The results of the harvest could swing the balance of life and death in the coming year, and so these first fruits of the earth were given thanks for and celebrated in a great feast to the god Lugh, and sacrifices were made in the hope of renewal for the following year.

OPPOSITE *The harvesting of crops was a rare time of plenty for the Celts.*

Good tidings:

sea fruitful,

shellfish plentiful,

woods smile,

fruit-trees ripening,

wheatfields grow,

bee-swarms are many,

a radiant world.

Kindly summer,

tidings good.

Irish, The Colloquy of the Two Sages, **tenth century**

Lughnasadh or the **Games of Lugh** takes place arund the time of the wheat harvest. As people began to rely more on calendar and clock time, the date was fixed, but originally, as a harvest festival, Lughnasadh would have taken place once the harvest had been collected. The harvest can vary by a few weeks between different parts of the Celtic world and according to the weather. Over the past few years, the local farmers have harvested the wheat around our home in Brittany on August Eve itself, but Welsh friends further north have not harvested until mid-August.

HARVEST

What seems on the surface a simple thing—an ear of wheat—has many powerful associations. Human invention of agriculture, like that of fire, was one of the great stepping stones in the advance of civilization. Once we learned to cultivate crops, our lives became much easier. We did not have to spend so much time searching for food as our hunter-gather ancestors who relied on meat, fish, roots, leaves, berries, and nuts for their sustenance.

Although the date can vary, Lughnasadh takes place when the Sun is in its own sign of Leo and at the fullness of its strength. The rays of the Sun from Midsummer onward dry out the green stalks and ears of wheat. The fields turn from fresh green to golden yellow-brown until the wheat is ready for reaping. The harvest is gathered and the wheat is threshed to produce sweet grain to be ground into flour for bread and strong stalks of straw for animal feed and bedding for the winter. This is a time of joy and celebration if the crop is good, but worry and anxiety if it is not.

RIGHT *The harvesting of corn in August is depicted here in a detail from the western facade of Chartres Cathedral, France.*

Not suprisingly, given the importance of wheat for survival, there are many traditions associated with its cutting. Often one corner of a field was left untouched, so a small part of the grain was offered back to the earth. The first sheaf would be set aside for making a special bread. Another sheaf might be kept in the house for luck, or in Scotland for making Bride dolls at Imbolc. Today, the fields around our home are cut by agricultural contractors, but the local farmer still comes before the machines to cut the first sheaf by hand and to take it home.

LUGH

The God Lugh was worshiped throughout the Celtic world and gave his name to the French city of Lyon. In Irish myth, like many solar heroes, Lugh slays the old king whose reign has become negative. In this case, the old king is Balor, Lugh's grandfather. Balor has shut himself away on an island and imprisoned his daughter Eithne because of a prophecy that his grandson would slay him. Eithne manages to bear sons, one of whom is Lugh. Balor casts them to the sea but Lugh survives and returns in adulthood to kill him.

Legend tells us that Lugh instituted the Lughnasadh festival in honor of his foster mother the Goddess Tailtu. Lugh is one of the most attractive deities in the Irish pantheon. He is a brilliant and many-skilled God—a harper, hero, poet, healer, and magician. His sacred weapon is a spear and he is sometimes known as Lugh the Light Bearer. The spear suggests his association with the rays of the Sun.

There were Lughnasadh festivals all over Ireland. Most festivals were dedicated to a local Goddess, possibly seen here as the giver of the harvest. Goods, cattle, and horses were traded. Young men and women went courting. Feasts were held and, most importantly in horse-crazy Ireland, there was racing and betting.

TELTOWN MARRIAGES

The largest Lughnasadh festival was at Teltown in County Meath. Teltown is the anglicized form of Tailtu. Until the twelfth century, Teltown was the site of the Aonach Tailteann Games. These were a kind of Irish Olympics similar to the Highlands Games held in Scotland today. Some customs from the Games continued until the nineteenth century. Teltown was famous for its "Teltown marriages." A couple could contract a Teltown marriage for a year and a day and then dissolve it if they wished. Given the Catholic Church's more restrictive marriage practices, Teltown marriages were popular.

A GODDESS FESTIVAL

Many Celtic traditions associated with goddess worship were in the Christian era put under the patronage of Mary, Bride, or one of the other female Celtic saints. In Brittany on July 26 there is a major celebration for St. Anne of Brittany whose cult center is situated at the site of the main shrine of the Pagan Goddess Ana. Further north in Scotland, the harvest was usually later and often festivities were combined with the feast of the Virgin Mary on August 15.

THE HARVEST LOAF

The first wheat of the harvest was baked into a special bread or cake. In the Highlands and Islands of Scotland, people went out into their fields in the early morning to pick ears of wheat to make the *Moilean Moire*, a bannock cake. The bannock was toasted on a fire of rowan or other woods associated with goddesses and magic. The father of the family broke the bannock and gave pieces to his wife and children in descending order of age. The family then sang a prayer of praise the *Iolach Mhoire Mhathar* or Praise Song of Mary Mother, while walking deosil around a fire. When this was complete, the fire embers and some pieces of old iron were placed in a pot. The father walked deosil around the house, and sometimes around the family's fields and flocks, singing the Praise Song of Mary as he went.

On the feast of Mary the fragrant,
Mother of the Shepherd of flocks,
I cut me a handful of new wheat,
I dried it gently in the Sun,
I rubbed it sharply from the husk,
with my own palms.

◆

I ground it in a hand mill on Friday,
I baked it on a piece of sheep skin,
I toasted it in a fire of rowan wood,
and I shared it with my people.

◆

I went deosil around my house,
in the name of Mary Mother,
who promised to preserve me,
who does preserve me,
and who will preserve me,
in peace, in flocks,
in righteousness of heart,
in labor, in love,
in wisdom, in mercy,
for the sake of Thy passion,
Thou Christ of grace,
who till the day of my death,
will never forsake me.

107

SACRIFICE AND DEATH

An important theme of Lughnasadh is sacrifice. In ancient times in many societies, the king was considered Divine. He must die at the peak of his powers so that his strength and energy might pass to the new king. In Celtic lore, as with many tribal peoples, the King had to be in perfect health and sound of limb. The King's marriage with the land meant that the power of life was vested in him. If his strength failed and his powers waned, then the land would become barren and the people would die. This idea is found in the Grail stories and the myth of the Fisher King.

Lughnasadh is traditionally associated with the ritual slaying of the King. His blood is spilled on the reaped fields thereby returning his power and life force to the land from which it came. The King voluntarily sacrifices himself to renew the Earth.

The death theme is present in other ways at Lughnasadh. The fields of ripe wheat are home to foxes, rabbits, and other small creatures of the fields. As the reapers cut inward from the outer edge of the fields to the inner, the animals are trapped at the center. Humans with cudgels, or more recently with guns, would wait for the animals to break cover and attempt to flee. Usually they failed and there was

meat for the pot, but there would also be blood on the wheat. In the midst of the summer sun, and tainting the grain of life, is the blood of death and sacrifice. In fields of the past, this reminder was present throughout the growing season. Untainted by chemical sprays, blood red poppies bloomed among the green and then golden wheat.

FACING CHANGE

Hopefully, we are not called upon to make such dramatic sacrifices as that of a sacrificial king, but in this myth, there is a message for us all. We must face change.

Middle age and death are part of life's realities. We must accept that, whatever our worldly achievements, at some point we must let them go. We will have to take a step forward into the unknown—the realm of death and the afterlife. This involves an inner sacrifice; letting go of all that we have gained in life and detaching ourselves from the past.

The cycle of seasonal festivals is a wheel that is ever-turning. If we understand this, we can adapt and change. We take each day as a gift, which is all the more precious because it is transient. We learn to extract hope, peace, and joy from a draft that is mixed inevitably with some bitterness.

Lughnasadh is a time of feminine transition. The themes of Lughnasadh are about letting go and moving onward in our life's journey. The Goddess at Lughnasadh is the bountiful Mother, but she is also the Crone. She is the wielder of the sickle who cuts down the beautiful wheatfields so that the grain can be transformed. From the death of the wheat, a new substance is born.

LEFT The theme of death at Lughnasadh is present in an ancient Breton practice, where drowned bodies were sought by means of a loaf of bread pierced with a lit candle. The lighted boat would reveal the whereabouts of the body.

LUGHNASADH CELEBRATIONS

CELEBRATIONS

In the Eleusinian Mysteries of ancient Greece, some say, an ear of wheat was shown to the initiate as the final revelation. What did this mean? If you can, go out into the countryside and pick an ear of wheat. Otherwise, buy some dried wheat from a store that sells dried flowers for floral displays.

Hold an ear of wheat in your hand and meditate upon it. What does it tell you? How does it feel? The ripened ear of wheat has not the smoothness of youth, but the ripeness of age. It is dry, but has the promise of transformation. New life can spring from it; for within it is the seed. Within the seed is the promise of reincarnation and rebirth. This was the secret revealed to the initiate: we are born, we live, we die, and we live again.

LETTING GO OF ANGER

In order to move forward we have to let go. There are many ways in which we can become stuck in our lives and refuse to move forward. One way of becoming "stuck" is to hold on to anger. Lughnasadh Eve or dawn on Lughnasadh morning is a time to discard the outworn past in the same way as the outer husks of wheat are discarded. If you have suffered wrongdoing and still feel anger, this is a good time to leave this feeling in the past.

Take a piece of recycled or other natural paper that is biodegradable. Write down all that you want to put behind you. Now go out into your yard or go for a hike somewhere in a park or the countryside. Take fresh springwater with you, either water you have collected from a clean stream or river or bought water, a small clean towel, a gardening trowel, and some salt. Use rock salt or sea salt rather than salt treated with iodine.

Find a place in the earth to bury your paper where it will not be disturbed. Dig a hole. Sterilize the hole by sprinkling it with salt. Tear up your paper into small pieces and place it in the hole, saying as you do so:

I rid myself… (of anger, hurt, resentment to the past).

Say this as often as you wish as you dispose of your paper. When you have finished, wash your hands in the water saying:

May this water rid me of the negativity that has held me back.

Dry your hands, then sprinkle more salt over the paper saying:

With this salt I neutralize the negativity that has held me back. It is dead and gone.

Fill the hole with earth again. Gather your belongings and walk away from the hole without once looking back. You have let go.

BUILDING UP

Having got rid of any negativity, Lughnasadh is a good time to bring positive energy into your home. Make a seasonal altar as near the center of your home as possible. Cover the altar with a gold or orange altar cloth to remind you of the baking heat of the Sun. Decorate your altar with wheat mixed with red flowers and with golden yellow candles.

The foods of Lughnasadh are products made of wheat—cakes or bread and ale. If you have never baked bread, now is a good time to try. This recipe was taught to my friend Marie by her Irish grandmother.

SODA BREAD

• 1 lb all-purpose flour (or a mixture
of all-purpose and wholewheat flour)
• salt
• 1/2 teaspoon cream of tartar
• 1/2 teaspoon bicarbonate of soda
• 1/2 pint milk
• 1 tablespoon vinegar

Light two
candles

RIGHT **Give thanks at
Lughnasadh by placing homemade bread on your altar.**

1. *In a large mixing bowl, place 1lb of all-purpose flour or a mixture of all-purpose and wholewheat flour.*

2. *Add a large pinch of salt, plus half a teaspoon each of cream of tartar and bicarbonate of soda.*

3. *In a jug, mix half a pint of milk with a tablespoon of vinegar.*

4. *Add the milk and vinegar mixture to the flour a little at a time, until you have a dough.*

5. *Knead the dough a little, then shape it into a round lump. Cut an equal armed cross on the top.*

6. *Bake the loaf in a hot oven for 35-40 minutes.*

If you would prefer a sweet version, add some sugar and raisins to the dough.

BLESSING THE HOME

Besides bringing new energy into your home, you may want to protect it by a simple blessing rite. This is no substitute for a burglar alarm, but it is a useful addition that sends out a subliminal message: this place is protected, do not disturb.

You will need a bowl of springwater and a small bowl of salt. Place these on your altar and light two candles. On your altar, place your loaf and a goblet of ale or some fruit juice to bless later.

With clean hands, place your fingertips in the water and visualize a golden stream of light and energy flowing down your hands into the water. You might like to play some soothing music while you do this. When you feel you have done enough, ask for a blessing on your water. You could ask here in the name of Ana, Great Mother Goddess and later patron saint of the Celts of Brittany.

Sprinkle some of the salt into the bowl of water. Now take the bowl of blessed water around each room of your home. As you enter each room, ask the Gods to bless your home and to make it a place of peace and your own personal sanctuary. Sprinkle a little water around the edge of each room. Walk around the rooms clockwise starting from the door. Sprinkle the threshold of the doorway as you go out of the room. As you sprinkle your blessed water, think about its protective energy filling the room and safeguarding its outer boundaries. If you can sprinkle water around the outside of your home as well, so much the better. It is best to avoid sprinkling the salted water on metal.

When you have finished, pour any remaining water on the Earth, or set it aside and take it outside later. It is good spiritual practice to treat with respect anything we use for a sacred purpose. Do not just throw the remains of your water down the sink! Now bless your loaf and ale or some other drink as symbols of the bounty of the Earth. Place your hands on the bread and bless your loaf as you blessed food at Midsummer.

O Queen of Earth and Heaven

bless this food for our bodies

bestow upon us health, wealth, and the joy of life

which is perpetual happiness.

If there are others celebrating with you, pass bread around with a greeting:

Blessing of Lughnasadh to you!

Now bless your drink in your own words.

CORN DOLLIES

Another traditional way of protecting the home was to make corn dollies from the first stems of wheat. These were not dolls but woven charms of wheat which hung on the walls or above door-ways and windows to bring blessings to the house. If you can obtain wheat, in addition to your protection ceremony for your home, you might like to sit down at the end of your Lughnasadh rite to make a corn dolly. Opposite, is my friend Marie's description of one type of corn dolly.

ABOVE Corn dollies, made from the first stems of harvested wheat, were believed to protect the home until the following year's harvest.

TO MAKE A CORN DOLLY

Take 13 long stems of wheat. Cut them to equal length.

You will also need five or ten spare stems without ears.

Tie the 13 stems together tightly, just below the ears.

Take the eight middle stems. Tie them at the far end, leaving about 7 inches free.

Hold your bunch of wheat upside down, so the ears are pointing downward.

This will leave you with a central bunch and five loose stems around the outside. Spread the five loose stems horizontally in five directions.

Point one of them toward you; this is stem no. 1. The others are numbered stems 2, 3, 4, 5 in a clockwise direction. Now begin to braid them.

Take stem no. 1 and lay it over no. 2. Take stem 2 and lay it over stem 3. Take stem 3 and lay it over stem 4. Take stem 4 and lay it over no. 5. And so on.

You will find that although you are working with five stems, you are forming a square around the central bunch of eight. As you continue, your woven stems will spiral up and around the central bunch in a pleasing manner.

As your original stems grow too short to braid further, join them to your spare stems. You will find that the centers are hollow and you will be able to insert one inside the other. One addition to each of the five stems should be enough, but if your stems are short, you may need to use two.

Continue braiding. When your spiral reaches the top end of the central bunch, carry on, but lay the stems you have been braiding ever closer together in the spiral, so they close up over the ends of the central bunch.

Braid the remainder, until you have used up all your stems. Fold the braid over and tie it with red ribbon leaving a loop at the top to hang the dolly up.

FALL EQUINOX

A second harvest of fruit and vegetables took place at the time of the Fall Equinox, and was accompanied by more feasting and celebrating. As with the Spring Equinox, this was a time when day and night were of equal length and nature in perfect balance. It was a transitional point in the year, and as summer receded, the gods of the approaching winter were welcomed and honored.

OPPOSITE *Autumn is a transitional point in the year and this is marked by the changes in color all around us, from greens and yellows, to reds and golds.*

A good season for staying is autumn;

there is work then for everyone before

   the very short days.

Dappled fawns from amongst the hinds,

the red clumps of the bracken shelter them;

stags run from the knolls at the belling of

   the deer-herd.

Sweet acorns in the wide woods,

stubble around the wheatfields over the

   expanse of brown earth.

There are thornbushes and prickly

   brambles

by the midst of the ruined court;

the hard ground is covered with heavy fruit.

Hazelnuts of good crop fall from the huge

   old trees on dykes.

Irish, attributed traditionally to Amergin,

eleventh century

The Autumn or Fall Equinox is known in Druidry as *Alban Elued*. The autumn is the time of the last fruit and vegetable harvests of the year. Grain must be threshed and foodstuffs placed in store for the winter. This was a crucial time of reckoning. Was there enough food for the winter? Were all the storehouses full or would there be famine?

The Lughnasadh wheat harvest provided bread, the staff of life. The September fruit and vegetable harvest provided the vitamins essential for maintaining health through the winter. In the Highlands and Islands of Scotland, vegetables such as carrots, which grow well in sandy soil beside the sea, were so prized that they were given as autumn gifts with good wishes and blessings.

RIGHT *The deer was a significant animal to the Celtic people, whose very existence was so dependent on agriculture and hunting*

MANANNÁN AND MICHAEL

In the Celtic world during the fall, the night mists come in from the sea to cover the land. It is the time of high tides and gales, a time of danger. In Gaelic tradition, the God of the Sea was Lir. Lir's son who protected sailors and fishermen was Manannán mac Lir, the Son of the Sea. Waves are often described in Celtic poetry as white mares and in Celtic myth and legend the sea god Manannán is often closely associated with horses.

PRAYER TO MICHAEL

Thou Michael the Victorious,
I walk beneath thy shield;
thou Michael of the white steed
and of the brilliant blades,
conqueror of the dragon,
be thou at my back;

◆

Thou ranger of the heavens,
O Michael the Victorious, my pride and
my guide,
O Michael the Victorious, the glory of
mine eye.

◆

I walk in the company of my saint,
on the plain, on the meadow,
on the cold heathery hill.
Though I should travel the ocean
and the hard edge of the world,
no harm can ever before me
'neath the shelter of thy shield.

O Michael the Victorious, jewel of my heart,
O Michael the Victorious, God's shepherd
thou art.
Be the Sacred Three of Glory
aye at peace with me,
with my horses, with my cattle,
with my wooly sheep in flocks,
with the crops growing in the field,
or ripening in the sheaf;
on the plain, on the moor,
in cole, in heap, or stack.

◆

Every thing on high or low,
every furnishing and flock,
belong to the Holy Triple One of Glory,
and to Michael the Victorious.

In Celtic Christianity, many of Manannán's attributes were absorbed by St. Michael. The most important sites for churches dedicated to St. Michael were on coastal sites—St. Michael's Mount in Cornwall, Mont Ste. Michel in Brittany and Aird Michael in Uist. In Scotland, St. Michael was called Brian Michael or God Michael. His feast day is just after the Equinox on September 29. Together with Bride's festival at Imbolc, it was one of the greatest feast days.

JOURNEYING TO
THE OTHER WORLD

In Scottish tradition, it was St. Michael's task to convey dead souls to the Otherworld. In Breton tradition, this is the task of the Ankhou. He is a skeletal figure who drives a creaking horsedrawn coach which comes out of the waves through the sea mists to convey the dead to the Otherworld.

The **Otherworld** or **Tir na N'Og**, plays an important part in Celtic myth. It was a beautiful realm of warmth and Nature in abundance; a perpetual early summer heady with the smell of flowers and blossom. It was filled with the sound of bird song and tinkling streams. It is a land in which nothing grows old and there is no disease. To enter the Otherworld is to enter Paradise—a brighter,

ABOVE *St. Michael's Mount in Cornwall is separated from the mainland at high tide. St. Michael is said to be a later incarnation of Manannan mac Lir, Celtic god of the sea.*

more beautiful version of the mundane world. Death held no fear.

The Otherworld was also the home of otherworldly beings, the fairy folk. In more recent tales, fairies are described as tiny beings that we can hold on the palm of our hands, but this is a new idea. Originally, fairies were beings who looked like mortals but were more beautiful and alluring. They also possessed magical powers.

TAM LIN

At special times and at certain places, mortals could enter the Otherworld, to dwell there for a while and then return. The Scottish story of Tam Lin is one of the better-known tales and has been popularized in recent decades by folk groups. Tam Lin is a knight who is captured by the Queen of Fairy and becomes her consort in the Otherworld. Tam Lin is not faithful to the Queen of Fairy. He can reenter the mortal world for short periods and when wandering in the woods, he encounters Janet, a mortal noblewoman, and makes her pregnant. Tam Lin seems happy with his Fairy Queen and mortal mistress until he learns that he is to rule for only seven years. At the end of his seven-year reign, he is to be slain as a sacrificial king. Tam Lin tells Janet of his predicament and, like a good enterprising Celtic woman, she decides to defy the Queen of Fairy and to rescue him. Janet goes through a terrifying ordeal. The Queen of Fairy shape-changes Tam Lin into a snake and other frightening creatures, but Janet holds him tightly until at last he resumes his mortal form. Janet then takes him home to do his fatherly duty.

TURNING INWARD

As we approach Equinox, the days grow shorter and the nights colder, until on the day of the Equinox itself the hours of daylight equal the hours of light. We are poised at a changing of a tide. In spring and summer, the impetus of the life force is outward toward activity and creation. The autumn is a time for reflection and study. We turn inward as the nights draw in and the outside world holds less appeal.

The Equinox takes place at the transition of Virgo and Libra. Virgo is an Earth sign and the astrological sign that presides over agriculture. We leave Virgo as the last harvests end. We enter Libra, an Air sign, and turn to the things of the mind. In most countries, academic semesters begin around late August or September. This reflects the requirements of agricultural societies where children were needed in the summer to work on the farms. The thirty-acre farm where I lived as a child had few machines and one of my favorite summer treats was to help with haymaking and harvest. There are practical reasons for the academic calendar, but it also makes psychological, spiritual, and astrological sense to focus on the things of the mind and spirit as we approach Libra.

A NEW QUEST

Spring and summer are about the outer world and the challenges and goals of youth. In autumn, we turn to the inner world and spiritual realm and the challenges and goals of midlife and beyond. The Equinox tides and winds can bring storm and shipwreck. They are a time of transition. This is apparent in the world of Nature. Leaves fall from the trees, birds migrate, and all the signs of life disappear one by one. Some of these transitions are on the material plane. Others are spiritual transitions. The Mystery Initiations of Eleusis in Greece took place at this time.

At midlife, we often face enforced transition and change through being laid off or through children growing up and leaving home. At these times, we must examine our lives and values and decide whether an outward, worldly orientation is still sufficient for our happiness. We may reevaluate our chosen profession; perhaps by looking at more spiritually satisfying careers or by returning to further study to renew and update our approach to our current job.

For those on a spiritual path, autumn is a good time to turn inward and examine our dedication to our chosen path. We may find that it is time to make or renew our spiritual quest. Sometimes this can take us into new spiritual pathways. Alternatively, we may remain in the tradition of our birth, but reexamine our role in it; perhaps making a spiritual retreat to renew the wellsprings of inspiration within us.

RIGHT The Celtic Otherworld was a paradaisical realm inhabited by fairies and sacred animals. It was a place to be anticipated with joy, not feared.

SEERSHIP

As the nighttime world comes to dominate the year, it is time to develop our spiritual and psychic awareness. At Samhain we divine for ourselves. The Equinox tide is when we seek prophecy from others. In the ancient Celtic world, those with "the sight" were greatly revered. No important action could take place without consulting them.

The voice of the seer can be interpreted as the warning voice of the unconscious, whose time frame is often ahead of that of the conscious mind. In the famous Ulster story from the Táin bó Cuailnge or Cattle-raid of Cooley, Medb or Maeve Queen of Connacht is planning a raid on Ulster. A beautiful golden-haired young woman approaches her riding in a chariot. She is dressed in rich garments and armed as a warrior. Maeve, seeing herself as a Queen and the woman's social superior, demands to know who she is.

"I am Fedelma and I am
a poetess of Connacht."

◆

"Where have you come from?"

◆

"From learning verse and vision in Scotland."

◆

"Have you the sight?"

◆

"Yes, I have."

◆

"Then look for me and see,
what will befall my army.
Fedelma, prophetess,
how seest thou my warrior host?"

◆

"I see it crimson, I see it red.
I see a battle:
a golden-haired man with much blood about his belt
and the light of a hero around his head.
His brow is full of victories.
Whole hosts he destroys,
the bodies pile up in massacre,
in thousands you yield your heads.
I am Fedelma. I hide nothing."

Fedelma has seen the Ulster hero Cú Chulainn who will defeat Maeve's army. Unfortunately for Maeve, like many an impetuous Celt before and after her, she ignores the warning of the prophetess.

The Equinox is a good time to seek guidance from others. We may know a good astrologer, clairvoyant, or tarot reader who can give us insights into the year to come. Alternatively, we might prefer to seek spiritual guidance from a spiritual leader or teacher who is further along our chosen path than ourselves.

RETREATS

There are many organizations offering retreats. You can find information in New Age magazines. These will list New Age, Native American, Buddhist, and Celtic Pagan retreats, and also courses and workshops. Catholic and other Christian book

ABOVE *Stags, along with other horned-god figures, were very closely associated with the Celtic Otherworld, and were able to lead people in and out of this realm.*

stores will have magazines and information about the various Christian retreat centers. Events exploring Celtic Christianity are becoming increasingly common in many Catholic, Episcopalian, and Unitarian centers.

Most spiritual retreats are organized by a particular tradition, but they are usually open to people of all faiths. Spiritual wisdom is universal. It may manifest in different forms in different cultures, but there are certain eternal truths which are common to all traditions. We can choose to go to a center that follows our own faith, but it can be equally enlightening, perhaps even more so, to learn how other traditions convey their spiritual teachings.

Most retreats have common practices regardless of their tradition. These involve silence, medita-

tion, perhaps spiritual reading and the opportunity for guidance and advice from a spiritual leader or teacher. Retreats are often conducted in settings of great natural beauty. These can precipitate spiritual insights in themselves.

There are also other retreats and workshops that are not overtly spiritual, but which can assist us on our spiritual journey. You could look at retreats and workshops run by the more spiritually oriented schools of psychotherapy. New Age, psychology, and Christian retreat movement magazines will list these. Look for groups working from a transpersonal perspective or Jungian groups, based on the work of the famous psychologist Carl Jung. Carl Jung and his wife Emma had a deep interest in exploring the psychological wisdom of Celtic myth.

AUTUMN EQUINOX CELEBRATIONS

CELEBRATION

For your altar you will need a cloth that reminds you of the colors of autumn; colors such as orange, brown, or red. For decoration, look for bronze or orange colored flowers and leaves. You will also need two matching candles, one white and one black, or dark blue. Place the white candle on the right of your altar and the black candle on the left.

Floating candles represent the sun departing

RIGHT **Light your candles in a darkened room to give your rites their strongest effect**

You will also need a candle for floating on water. You can buy these in good candle stores. The custom of floating candles on water around fall is common to many cultures. It is a sign that the Sun is going away from us for a time. If you are near a lake, river, or the sea, you can float your candle outside. If not, you will need a bowl of water for your altar. Equinox rites should be quiet and meditative. Sunset or just after dark is a good time to begin. Light a taper and put out any lights in your room. Light first the white and then the black altar candles as you say these words.

At the turning of the year,
the light equals the darkness,
the balance of the hands is true,
energy and light, peace and night.

Sit down by your altar and review your spiritual life since last Samhain. What requests and wishes have you made? What has been granted and what has not? Are there good reasons in retrospect why some requests and wishes have not been answered? Has something better happened instead? Now you are approaching the last phase of your journey around the Year Wheel. What rites, prayers, and regular spiritual practice have you carried out? Could you do a little better in the year to come?

You might like to bless cakes or bread and wine as you did at Midsummer. Then, particularly if you have been outside, you might like some warming soup. Mushrooms are a traditional feast at this time of year. My friend Clare in Dublin, a wonderful cook, gave me this recipe. It was given to her by her mother.

WILD MUSHROOM SOUP

INGREDIENTS

to serve four:
- 1/2 cup mushrooms, dried
- 6 shallots, chopped
- 1 lb mushrooms, fresh
- 2 cloves garlic, chopped
- lemon thyme
- parsley, 1 bay leaf
- 4–5 juniper berries, crushed
- mushroom stock
- 1 glass red wine
- sour cream or yoghurt to serve
- puff pastry vol-au-vent cases, homemade or frozen
- cheese, finely grated, to serve

Cover the dried mushrooms in two pints of boiling water and leave them to soak for at least half an hour.

Strain and chop, reserving the liquid for stock.

Sauté the shallots in butter until transparent.

Add the fresh mushrooms and cook until just golden.

Add the garlic, lemon thyme, parsley, a bay leaf, juniper berries, and mushroom stock.

You might also like to add a glass of red wine for flavor.

Allow the mixture to simmer gently, uncovered, for about 45 minutes.

Serve in bowls.

Stir in soured cream or yoghurt and season to taste.

The wild mushroom mixture is also delicious seved in puff pastry vol-au-vent cases. Prepare these in advance. They can be homemade or frozen.

SOME INFORMATION AND SOURCES

Now you are on the last phase of your journey around the Year Wheel. If you would like to know more about the world of the Celts, here are some starting points.

BOOKS

• Welsh myth and legend is found in the Mabinogion. Try the Jeffrey Gantz translation published by *Penguin Books*, 1976.

• The Irish myth cycle of the Táin bó Cuailnge can be found in the translation of the Irish poet Thomas Kinsella, THE TÁIN, *Oxford University Press*, 1970 edn.

• Professor T.G.E. Powell's archaeological study THE CELTS, *Thames and Hudson*, 1980 edn., is a good introduction to ancient Celtic life.

• Dr. Miranda Green of the *University of Wales* has produced a beautifully illustrated introduction to modern and ancient Druidry: EXPLORING THE WORLD OF THE DRUIDS, *Thames and Hudson*, 1997.

• The world of Celtic Christianity is explored in Nigel Pennick's lovely book THE CELTIC SAINTS, *Thorsons*, 1997. Another fascinating book is Dr. Oliver Davies's and Dr. Fiona Bowie's CELTIC CHRISTIAN SPIRITUALITY: MEDIEVAL AND MODERN, *SPCK*, 1995.

DRUIDRY

If you are interested in Druidry, here are some starting points. All Druid groups are run by volunteers and have limited budgets. If you want a response, you must send postage stamps for inland correspondence or International Reply Coupons for overseas post. International Reply Coupons are available from large post offices. Do not send your own stamps to foreign countries. They cannot be used.

• ARN DRAIOCHT FEIN, PO Box 516, East Syracuse, NY 13057-0516; Web site—http://www.adf.org—is the largest North America Druid organization. ADF practices NeoPagan Druidism. It has a journal The Druid's Progress and offers training in Druidry.

• ASSEMBLÉS ARMORIQUE ATLANTIQUE DE LA TRADITION DES DRUIDES, c/o Michel Raoult, La Pommerie-Avalon, 29252 Plouezoc'h, France, can provide contact with Breton Druidry.

• INSTITUTE OF CORNISH STUDIES, Trevenson, Pool, Redruth, Cornwall, England, is a contact point for Cornish Celtic studies.

• ORDER OF BARDS, OVATES, AND DRUIDS, PO Box 1333, Lewes, BN7 3ZG, England; Web site–http://www .obod.co.uk—is the largest Druid order in Europe. It also has groups in North America. OBOD offers training in mythology, history, folklore, healing, and divination, through correspondence courses, workshops, camps, and retreats in Europe and the United States. The

Chosen Chief of the Order, Philip Carr-Gomm makes frequent visits to the United States and also runs an annual retreat on the sacred island of Iona off the coast of Scotland. OBOD has a members' magazine.

CELTIC CONNECTIONS

• If you would like to know more about Brittany, information is available in English or French on the Web site http://www.bretagne.com—which also has information about the InterCeltic festival at Lorient.

• My husband Chris and I run five-day retreats on Celtic Paganism each summer in Brittany. Information can be obtained by email from: bmdeosil@aol.com; or by post from: BM DEOSIL, London WC1N 3XX, England.

• For information on Ireland, a starting point is: http://www.paddynet.com/island/index.html.

• Further information on Celtic web sites and many links can be found on:http://www.geocities.com/~celtic – lore/links.html.

The blessings of Sun, sky, wave, and the warm Earth to you, and Good Luck on your journey!

INDEX

The publishers would like to thank the following for the use of pictures:

Archiv Für Kunst Und Geschicte, London: p. 29 (Dusseldorf Museum)
The Bridgeman Art Library: pp. 4/5 (Maas Gallery, courtesy of Arthur Rackham's family)
Dundee Museum and Art Gallery: p. 32
(John Duncan: Riders of the Sidhe, courtesy of John Duncan's Estate)
Fine Art Photographic Library: pp. 27,120
Fortean Picture Library: pp. 82; FPL/Janet and Colin Bord: pp. 2/3, 20
FPL/The Stock Market, London: pp. 16/17
Games System Inc., Stamford, Conn.: p. 71
Images Colour Library, London/Charles Walker Collection: pp. 8, 9, 13, 42, 43, 44, 58, 64, 70,
72, 80, 81, 85, 94, 105, 109, 118
National Museums and Galleries on Merseyside: p. 48 (Lady Lever Art Gallery, Port Sunlight)
The Stock Market, London: pp. 12, 14/15, 21, 25, 30, 34, 35, 41, 45, 47, 55, 56, 57, 60, 64, 67, 68, 69, 73, 75, 79,
88, 90, 93, 96, 103, 115, 116, 122